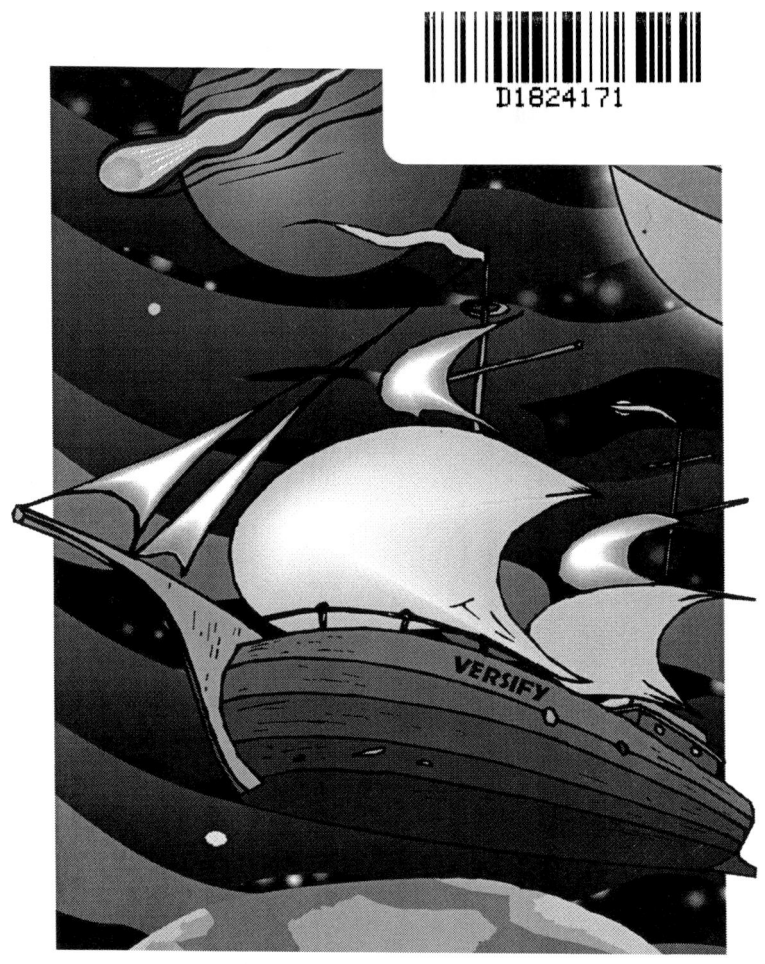

POETIC VOYAGES
WEST SUSSEX VOL I

by Dave Thomas

First published in Great Britain in 2001 by
YOUNG WRITERS
Remus House,
Coltsfoot Drive,
Peterborough, PE2 9JX
Telephone (01733) 890066

HB ISBN 0 75433 322 1
SB ISBN 0 75433 323 X

FOREWORD

Young Writers was established in 1991 with the aim to promote creative writing in children, to make reading and writing poetry fun.

This year once again, proved to be a tremendous success with over 88,000 entries received nationwide.

The Poetic Voyages competition has shown us the high standard of work and effort that children are capable of today. It is a reflection of the teaching skills in schools, the enthusiasm and creativity they have injected into their pupils shines clearly within this anthology.

The task of selecting poems was therefore a difficult one but nevertheless, an enjoyable experience. We hope you are as pleased with the final selection in *Poetic Voyages West Sussex Vol I* as we are.

CONTENTS

Kirsten Parnell	68
Sheran Owens	69
Vanessa Pitt	70
Christopher Kidd	70
James Forbes-King	71
Tom Grounds	72
Alice Brewer	73
Emma Alderman	73

Thornberry Middle School

Rosie Lynn	74
Natasha Woollacott	75
Crystal Mustchin	75
Hannah Potter	76
Martin Tullett	76
Lorna Sherriff	77
Stephanie Robinson	77
Kevin Withell	78
Darryl Clement	78
Kristina Adamson	79
Ayesha Travis	80
Parris Johnson	80
Lee Hayman	81
Katie Mellish	81
Emily Barton	82
Rhiannon Saunders	82
Simon Withell	83
Bryony Short	83
Charlotte Adsett	84
Daisy Adamson	84
Caroline Glockler	84
Lucy Minor	85
Nicole Skinner	85

Windmills County Junior School

| Benjamin Northrop | 86 |
| Nicole Gibson | 87 |

Sarah Hartley	87
Conor Hale	88
Miriam Kennedy	89
Daisy Marsh	89
Tom Richardson	90
Ashley Raim	91
Simon Bartlett	92
Paul Blackham	92
Abigail Elkins	93
Claire Elizabeth Varndell	93
Hayley Elphick	94
Joanna Griffin	94
Emma Hayter	95
Ryan Cannell	95
Emma Speer	96
Charlotte Rider	96
Danielle Page	97
Sam Hayter	97
Ellie Groves	98
David Chad	98
Naomi Morley	99
Emma Ingarfield	99
Jeffrey Liu	100
Eleanor K G Thomson	100
Sean Saunders	100
Hannah Logan	101
Sara Fullbrook	101
Lianne Baker	101
James Cassidy	102
Hayley Maloney	102
Fay Lewis	103
Kristina Scuse	103
Francesca Guratsky	103
Matthew Carter	104
Victoria Monson	104
Sophie Sutcliffe	104
Susan Bell	104

The Poems

POTION H²0 FORMULA

Eye of newt and toe of frog,
A lump of poison and a worm-eaten log,
Lip from a bear, wing of a vampire bat,
A pinch of powder and a whip of human fat.
Finger from a lion and a skunk's tail,
Hammer, hammer and in goes the rusty nail.
Puss of a spot and in goes the whole lot.

Double, double, toil and trouble, fire burn and cauldron bubble,

Rabbit's hair and pig's tail,
This potion will never fail!
Camel's hump, and lizard's tongue,
Snout of a hog and a wolf's lung,
Iguana's tail and a tiger's claw,
Elephant's trunk and sweets galore!
Horse's hoof and a dragon's eye,
An eagle's beak and a cat that can fly,
A stonefish's fin and a penguin's foot,
Some very fine sand and a lot of soot.

Double, double, toil and trouble, fire burn and cauldron bubble.

Stir around for seventeen days and add an orange basketball,
Then throw in an extra Barbie doll,
This potion will bring shivers and fatal illnesses throughout your body
Making you feel like you are upside down.
It will last exactly seventy-two hours and fifteen minutes
Until you drop dead and everyone will think you are sleeping.

Aayesha Haleem (11)

THE HOUSE IS WAITING!

The house is on its own
Waiting longingly
Please come home!
Please come home!
The doors creak mysteriously
Please shut me!
Please shut me!
The TV left on
Watching itself
Please watch me!
Please watch me!
The dripping of the tap
Bouncing onto the bottom of the sink
Please drink me!
Please drink me!
The bed's not made
Just lying there peacefully
Please make me!
Please make me!
The laundry is all alone
Just sitting there smelly and dirty.
Please clean me!
Please clean me!
The stereo left on
Just playing there dolefully
Please listen to me!
Please listen to me!
The letters fall through the letterbox
Please open me!
Please open me!

The house is on its own
Waiting longingly,
Please come home!
Please come home!

Piers Brown (11)
Ardingly College Junior School

WHEN THE HOUSE IS ALONE

Doors creaking slowly,
Clocks ticking endlessly,
Toys sitting bored stiff,
Teddy bears sitting lonely.
'Make me, make me!' shrieked the unmade bed,
Cushions sitting comfortably,
Phones ringing loudly,
Letters unopened,
Words in books messing about,
Unwashed crockery sulking,
Teacloths nattering amongst each other,
'Wash me, wash me!' pleaded the dirty underwear,
The smell of deodorant lingering in the air,
Clothes dancing in the washing machine,
Taps dripping slowly and quietly,
Radios singing tunefully,
Televisions buzzing with colours,
Newspapers urgently wanting to tell you the news,
Bloodsucking plasters dying of thirst,
Aerials fighting away the birds
And reflections in mirrors stolen.

Luke Smolinski (11)
Ardingly College Junior School

WHEN I'M NOT THERE

When I'm not there and the lights are off
The radio speaks quietly to itself
The dusty grey pillows resting on spare beds
Droplets of rain throw themselves onto the misty window
The log fire claps to call me back home
The telephone rings desperately
Outside the gutters dribble the rain
Cups and plates sobbing on the draining board
Careless dust flies through the air
The rug lies resting soon to be downtrodden
Children's toys deserted on the carpet
Mice rushing across the kitchen top
Water escaping from its pipe

When I'm not there
It's not what you think
It's not silent or still
It's alive.

Will Kidger (10)
Ardingly College Junior School

ALL THE HOUSE IS EMPTY

Doors creaking, taps leaking
Toilet flushing, water pipes rushing.
All the house is empty.
Wind blowing, weeds growing
All under my bed.

There are spiders and moles, moths and flies
Caterpillars and wasps!
But that's not all!

There's bats in the dark, my cat's in the car.
The house is a massive dump.

There are heaps of washing, plates that need washing
And ponging socks too!

When I'm not there the house isn't bare,
In fact it's really packed.

With horrible stuff that makes you feel rough
And it's pretty disgusting to me.

Don't you agree?

Joe Bott (10)
Ardingly College Junior School

THE DESERTED HOUSE

Floorboards happily laughing,
Cushions awesomely sighing,
Fluttering letters angrily fall through
The ferocious letterbox,
Doorbell ringing cheekily,
Grandfather clock
Ticking thoughtfully,
Tap dripping as if it's a race,
Cars zooming past joyfully,
Trickling water rushes through
The discarded squeaky pipe,
Cutlery stacked up hungrily,
Coats innocently hang
Beds unmade, sitting lonely,
Gusts of wind whistle aggressively,
Washing machine dancing
Merrily.

Tamsin Musgrave (10)
Ardingly College Junior School

BLANK AND BARE

Owls hoot from the beams,
Bill's shriek on the barren floor,
Howling winds wake the letter box,
Pages ruffle and shuffle in a book,
Rain comes hurtling through the discarded window,
Creaking stairs alert the cutlery,
Dust dawdles over to the abandoned pink cushions,
The stubborn dark green curtains bellow in the wind,
The grandfather clock chimes mournfully,
The overgrown ivy,
Bashes and crushes the tumbling wall,
As a haze of mist,
Sparkles, glitters then falls,
Before the creamy moon.

Kim Lewis (10)
Ardingly College Junior School

THE EMPTY HOUSE

The front door stands still longing for someone to turn its handle.
Letters lying patiently, waiting silently to be opened and read.
Along the narrow hallway the floorboards creak with the misery of
an empty house.
The dust floats carefree, ever silent, always watchful.
The phone rings, screaming madly for someone to talk to her.
The kitchen tap drips forgetfully.
The beds are standing untouched for them to comfort someone, anyone.
The books sit on the bookshelf, their emotions unknown.
Heaters turn on giving their warm and kind heat to an empty house.

Ivan Tcherkashnev (11)
Ardingly College Junior School

WHEN MY GRANDAD SLEEPS

When my grandad sleeps,
I'm sure he goes back to his old, English mansion
Into the picture of his lost, forgotten manor,
There was an old front door under a mottle and daub roof.
It creaks when it opens and exudes a cold, spooky draft.
He always stepped in and closed the door.
In that old house he felt like he was in a world of his own.
It was like stepping into nothingness.

The first source of light he could see was from a beautiful array
of windows,
Each one with its own story of wisdom and age.
A dark spiralling staircase,
Leading up into a vast gallery;
Old delicate chairs line its path.

A door with a frame, painted blue, with nails clumsily bashed in,
Holding on rough wooden letters,
Stating clearly that the following room belonged to
Graham Augustus Calviar.
In his shabby, cobwebby, dusty room
There was an old unmade bed,
Delicate bookshelves tightly packed with books ages old.
The shelves are all armed with precious ornaments,
Brass tennis medals, school trophies, a cracked Swiss army knife
and a youthful mirror.
I often try to imagine what it would be like to sleep in an old,
cracking, musty room,
With the bangs of the Second World War overhead.
I once did ask him what it was like,
But he just sighed and replied that it was like a dull, quiet,
black and white dream.

Owen Ridley (10)
Ardingly College Junior School

THE EMPTY HOUSE POEM

Pearly drops of water race down from the taps whooping with joy.
Water screams and scrambles as it is sucked into the bathroom plug.
The beer glass gives a cry as each precious drop of golden beer
Drips out into the deep dark bin.
In the kitchen a band strikes up as the wind blows
Pots and pans clash and clang merrily,
The others sit and sulk on the draining board.
The merciless washing machine whirls on, as the trapped clothes
Spin around in a colourful blaze, yelping
While the clothes try to escape this monster
That makes giant waves leap on them.
The tortuous dishwasher closes its door
And helpless crockery and cutlery moan
As they are half drowned in soapy water.
Unmade beds disco in the attic,
Their quilted fabric heaving in and out as the beds puff and pant.
The ancient chest of drawers heave in and out
Making a sound like an old church organ.
Downstairs the doorbell laughs cheekily
And footsteps stomp away grumpily.
A glass of water jumps off a shelf,
Smashing itself on the floor with hundreds of tiny glass splinters
Glinting menacingly on the clean kitchen floor.
Wet clothes dangle on the washing line,
Clinging on for dear life.

Caitlin Botha (10)
Ardingly College Junior School

A POEM, WHEN YOU ARE NOT THERE

The sound of dripping taps yelling 'Turn me off,' fill
The abandoned bathroom.
The cups snoozing in the sunlight on the wet draining board.
The CD 'Now 46' blaring away upstairs as the teddies have a disco.
The beds shouting 'Make me! Make Me!'
The washing falling out of the basket in a strop.
The dishwasher draining out its dirty coloured water.
And the dishes screaming 'Let me out I can't breathe!'
The house plants are in a temper, as they haven't been watered.
Dommy the dog shredding the newspaper, which was boasting
It was the best.
Lightning strikes as the cat knocks over the full water bowl.
Clock strikes 1.00pm.

Rosemary Rawlinson (10)
Ardingly College Junior School

I LEFT HOME THIS MORNING

Telephone ringing,
Someone knocking on the door,
Mice running,
Floorboards squeaking.
The boiler and radiators dripping cold water,
Dirty cups screaming
'Clean me! Clean me!'
Clocks ticking endlessly,
Cars zooming past.
Gusts of wind trying to hide the sound
Of next-door's television mumbling through the walls.
An Everest of shirts waiting to be ironed.
Our empty house - just waiting for us to come back.

Douglas Armstrong (10)
Ardingly College Junior School

MY RETURN TO THE HOUSE

The squeak of the grumpy door as it swings open to admit me.
There are taps dripping upstairs like they're best friends chatting.
The telephone bill is laughing on the doormat.
The drunk ringing of the wind chimes.
A death-watch beetle continually rapping its head on the roof beams.
The smell of mouldy discarded Cheddar cheese.
An unmade bed yelling 'Make me, make me!'
A phone ringing - urgent, urgent!
A blue tit singing merrily somewhere in a tree.
A knock on the door and then the crunch of gravel as they walk off.
A crash of glass as the neighbour's football makes a rather
dramatic entrance.
The video player gets stuck on the same line 'I'll get you! I'll get you!
I'll get you!'
The bored dust sitting on the window sill.
Homework lies unfinished on the kitchen table.
A fire place that looks like a grave.

Thomas Wilkins (11)
Ardingly College Junior School

EMPTY HOUSE

If I didn't live in my house it's something very upsetting
My room would actually be tidy and my dad would not be betting
The bread would not be mouldy and the sugar wouldn't be hard
The biscuits would not be stale and my mum wouldn't lose
her credit card
My sister wouldn't be mad but as far as I know
From my feet to my ears she was already mad before I came here
The next-door neighbours wouldn't be swearing
Because I got a higher mark in school by squaring.

Christopher Lew Kum Hoi (10)
Ardingly College Junior School

MY HOUSE

A lonely place is my house
When I am far from home.
The spoons are silent,
Crockery makes no sound,
Time does not move.

A lonely place is my house
When I am far from home.
The wind moans sorrowfully,
Rain patters against
The window of my empty house.

A lonely place is my house
When I am far from home.
A cat mews at my door,
Mice nibble at cheese,
Dogs bark at each other
In another street.

A lonely place is my house
When I am far from home.
The quilts untidily flung back,
Waiting patiently to be made,
The cushions sulking in the corner of the settee,
Wanting in the family home.

A lonely place is my house
When I am far from home.
And now I stand here
In front of you and really
Do wonder what happens
At the place I call home
While I am away.

Laurence Ashcroft (10)
Ardingly College Junior School

THE SLEEPING HOUSE

The house is sleeping but not inside,
All the objects are alive.
There's the ruffled bed screeching 'Make me!'
The golden sunlight pushing through the curtains,
Water attacking its way through the glimmering silver tap
Falling out
Splat!
    Splat!
        Splat!
          Splat!
The phone's ringing,
Saying 'Pick me up!' 'Urgent!'
No one is there to pick it up.
The cat is creeping through the hallway,
As quiet as a mouse,
As agile as a bird swooping through the forest
And as sleek as a slithering snake,
Abandoned books left open by a child.

So when you leave your house,
Do not think it's as quite as a mouse!

Matthew Marsh (11)
Ardingly College Junior School

WHAT AM I?

I am tall and I hope I never fall.
Creatures live on me, in my view there is lots to see.
When it is a sunny day, under me sometimes children play.
I have lots of bark, and I see owls when it is dark.
Do you know what is the word for me?
Yes, that's right, I am a tree!

Becky Jones (8)
Chesworth Junior School

THE ROLLER COASTER RIDE

Get in,
Belt up,
Get ready for a scary ride.
It starts,
It goes,
Down, round,
Until you get dizzy.
It flies like a bird,
But then it comes to a big drop.
You go through a dark tunnel, and through the mist.
Then they see a red light,
Everyone screams, they pass the red light.
They see the *stop* sign,
'Quick, I feel sick!'

Aaron Neale (7)
Chesworth Junior School

THE DAY JUST GONE

The moon is like a giant shooting star,
Its bright face makes the world look afar.
As it fades the world comes alive.
People out of their houses, bees out of their hives.
The sun's brilliant colours make the world look around,
As it reaches from the sky right down to the ground.
As the sun goes down late in the day,
People go in and stop their play.
As the moon rises up again, so bright,
All the people below shout, 'Goodnight!'
As I lay in bed the night drifts on,
Deep asleep I dream of 'The day just gone.'

Kieran Greig (10)
Chesworth Junior School

IPUMUS

I'll tell you about Ipumus,
A seemingly magical world,
For one side of it is always hot,
The other is always cold!

Ipumus never turns round and round,
Never, ever, that's right!
On one side of it, it's always day,
On the other, it's always night!

Ipumus is a proper planet,
It goes round a star called Tau Boo,
It also looks a bit like Earth,
For it's coloured green and blue.

There! I have finished my lecture,
I hope you now see
What a wonderful place Ipumus
Is to be!

Alice Broadribb (8)
Chesworth Junior School

SUMMER DAYS

I like summer days because . . .
It is warm, you can play outside
The sun is bright and the grass is green
The fields are yellow and the corn is ripe.

I like summer days because . . .
The clouds are white and the sky is blue
The playground shines from the glistening sunshine
The farmer is on his tractor combining the field.

I like summer days because . . .
The flowers bloom up from the soil
I like the smell of the colourful flowers all around us
The birds sing beautiful songs in the trees.

Rachel Banks (9)
Chesworth Junior School

HOMEWORK

The day has come for my dreaded enemy
To visit my tree house once again,
Homework, oh no not homework,
'Please don't give me homework.'

Please anything but homework,
I'll do simply anything for you,
I'll even be your slave for a whole week,
'Please don't give me homework.'

This week it's English,
A poem, brilliant, *not!*
I can't write poems,
'Please don't give me homework.'

What can I write it about?
I know I could write . . . no.
How about . . . it's too hard.
'Please don't give me homework.'

'Is that your homework?'
'Yeh, it's supposed to be.'
'That's superb Robert,
You're a poet and you didn't know it.'

Robert Hoskins (10)
Chesworth Junior School

THE CHANGES OF THE DAY

Birds singing softly like a choir,
Slightly out of tune.

A plane roaring like a dragon,
Letting nobody else into his spacious den of clouds.

Drops of crystal form on the grass,
A spectacular array of colour.

Terraced houses opposite have waves for roofs,
And the funnels of sinking ships for chimneys.

A vast sheepskin blanket covers the sky.

Murky grey patio,
A bleak memory of summer.

Wind unleashing all its anger
On the helpless trees below.

Showers of leaves fall from the trees,
Creating a yellow carpet on the lawn.

Choir practice over now.

Adam Manning (11)
Chesworth Junior School

MY TEDDY

My teddy loves me
He's cuddly and soft
He makes me feel happy
When I am sad and lost.

I tell him my secrets
And he swears he won't tell,
He's the captain of my room
And guards it well.

I love him to pieces
I'll keep him forever
Just me and my teddy
Together forever.

Luke Gooch (10)
Chesworth Junior School

MY BROTHER TOBY

My brother Toby
He is nearly three.
My brother Toby
He is not as tall as me.

My brother Toby
He is a poorly boy
But that does not stop him
Being a naughty boy.

My brother Toby
He plays trains
I build his railway
And he breaks it up.

My brother Toby
He is a pickle pot.
My brother Toby
I love him a lot.

If I had three wishes
One of them would be -
To make Toby better
For Mummy, Daddy and me.

Sebastian Turner (7)
Chesworth Junior School

THE CHOCOLATE WORLD

The chocolate world
I enter and I cannot believe my eyes,
My garden, my house, all chocolate!
I can taste it melting in my mouth.
I am there, all alone in this wonderful world.
It is like a dream come true, the prize of a lifetime.

The chocolate world
My body is paralysed, my brain is dead,
I know I am breathing, although I can't feel it.
The air is filled with the sweet smell of chocolate,
Is it a dream or is it real, I do not know, I must find out,
I touch the fine, smooth coating, now I know it's definitely real!

The chocolate world
I cannot resist any longer,
The temptation is too strong,
I take my first bite - delicious!
A couple more, until I can't stop.
The next thing I know this chocolate world has ended, all gone!

Jordan Kennedy (11)
Chesworth Junior School

THE STORM

The darkness of the storm blocks out the light,
Causing brightness to melt away.
Big and bulky clouds across the sky,
The storm has arrived!

Flashes of lightning light up the world,
Thunder *booms,* causing fright,
Rain falls out of the darkened clouds,
The wind blows across the deep heavens.

The clouds break away showing the bright sun,
The light is killing the darkness,
The cheerful clouds take over the sky,
The storm has gone at last.

Shaun Denman (9)
Chesworth Junior School

THE SNAIL TRAIL

I wake up, slowly I creep out of my hard, spiral shell.
My aim is to get to the garden shed by nightfall.
I fall out of the pot I sleep in, onto the concrete path.
Ready, steady, go . . .
I am gradually slithering across the path
Until I reach a stick.
Oh no, this journey is going to take longer than I thought,
I divert round the stick.
I'm off on the next part of my journey,
Over the grass.
I slide over the tickly blades
Leaving a slimy gunge wherever I go.
Ahhhhhh.
A tribe of ants march by causing me to stop.
Suddenly big, huge droplets of water start to fall.
I come across a pool of water.
What shall I do?
I know, I'll swim across.
No, I can't swim!
Ah ha, I know
I will try to get round the puddle before it gets bigger.
I manage to slither around there but . . .
I am losing time it will soon be dark.
What shall I do? Will I ever get there?

Abigail Cawston (10)
Chesworth Junior School

MY TRUE STORY

When I tried it I realised I was too small
That all of a sudden I had grown too tall
This is silly, how can it be?
I can't be too tall for it, not me.

I tried again but it was still the same
All I did was moan and complain
So my mum suggested that I should save up
So all my pocket money was put in a cup.

I saved and saved, it was hard for me
My mum said you can do it, you see
It took me ages but I got there
With a little help from my parents, I think that is fair.

So we went to the shop to have a look
I picked one out from a catalogue book
I must say it was a terrible hike
But I finally got it, my new bike.

Joe Lucas (9)
Chesworth Junior School

THE HORSE'S DREAM

I am a horse, I'm perfectly still
Collecting dust on the window sill
I stare out the window and wish I was free
I see running children and wish it were me

I'm here in the misty morning, I'm here in the neon night
I watch the sun rising and watch the moon bright
I wish for a jockey to ride me away
I'll never come back for at least one day

I dream one day I will be in a race
Galloping forward at my fastest pace
The man at the side shouts go, go go!
Before I know it my jockey yells whoa!

I hear people mention their win on the bet
I am the proudest with my bright blue rosette
I am a horse, I'm perfectly still
Collecting dust on the window sill.

Toby Fifield (10)
Chesworth Junior School

JIMMY BEAN

There was a little robot, his name was Jimmy Bean.
He went so fast along the road
he hardly could be seen.
His head was made of tin,
his body was made of steel
and at the end of every day, he ate a great big meal.

His greatest wish in all the world -
a girlfriend of his own.
He'd had enough of dreary days and nights so all alone.
He washed his hair,
he oiled his cogs, he shone his little wheels
and off he went along the road not knowing how love feels.

The robot nightclub was the place
he planned to meet a lovely girl.
He did a dance, he did a jerk, he did a great big swirl.
There she was, this shining star,
a girl who made him shake.
He took her arm and off they went, a perfect couple they did make.

Lauren Harding (9)
Chesworth Junior School

THE VOLCANO IS VICIOUS

The volcano is vicious,
It spits its poisonous ash
And dribbles its red spit.

The volcano is vicious,
It makes sculptures out of its molten clay
And preserves them for years.

The volcano is vicious,
It fries people alive
And they scream in terror.

The volcano is vicious,
It puffs its last puff
And dies out like thunder.

Thomas Fletcher (10)
Chesworth Junior School

LAVA RUN

It shoots out splashes of lava,
like a gushing waterfall.
It destroys everything in its path,
the mighty lava.
While it moves along,
a new age is dawning.
There is no way of stopping
this deadly monster with its fire of terror.
Into the sea it goes,
setting hard as rock.
The volcano.
Another new beginning,
not the end.

Jordan Moores (8)
Chesworth Junior School

MY BATTLE

My king and queen I save,
I move my pawn up two,
My bishop's gone to sleep,
So I move my horsey through.

The bishop's still asleep
My castle he is boring,
I need some peace to concentrate
Wish bishop would stop snoring!

Now it's my turn says the blacks,
I'll move my pawn up one,
Now I'll move my horsey through,
My gosh where has he gone?

Drat he has been taken,
By the ugly queen,
She got in gear and kicked his rear,
And now he can't be seen.

The blacks they are outnumbered,
But what is that I see?
A clearing for their king,
No, it can't be.

'It is,' cries Queeny,
A clearing for their king,
She races past all the cast,
Down the left wing.

Hooray, we shout in glory,
The blacks just have become,
The champions of the chessboard,
Hooray, we have just won.

Lewis Humble (10)
Chesworth Junior School

ROSE

The rose is delicate
It stands there bravely
Through rain and shine

The rose is delicate
It dances swiftly
Like a beautiful ice skater

The rose is delicate
It whispers silently
As it creeps through the grass blades

The rose is delicate
It pours silky syrup
Out of its soft petals

The rose is delicate
It walks carefully
Round pretty flower beds

The rose is delicate
It smiles up
At little kiddies' faces

The rose is delicate
It starts to creep
Back through the grass blades

The rose is delicate
A little tear of rain
Falls into its cup of life

The rose is delicate
Its soft petals
Start to fall

The rose is delicate
It lies there
With no life left to live

Vicky Yeoell (10)
Chesworth Junior School

WITCHES RIDING

Shut your windows,
Lock your doors,
For tonight the witches will ride.

Light a pumpkin
Outside your door,
For tonight the witches will ride.

Black cloaks they wear,
And pointed black hats,
For tonight the witches will ride.

For pets they have
Familiar black cats,
For tonight the witches will ride.

Hear them cackle,
In the middle of the night,
For tonight the witches will ride.

Victoria Paterson (8)
Chesworth Junior School

THE SHINING SUN

The shining sun
A bright yellow creeping up the edge of the world,
Like a monster unleashing all its energy.

The shining sun
A glistening star shimmering in the sky,
Like a powerful torch beaming across continents.

The shining sun
A solar ray burning as the Earth encircles it,
In its rage it spits out flames.

The shining sun
A blazing orange gas surrounding it,
Like a strong collision of hoops.

The shining sun
A blast of heat crushing nearby space cruisers,
Hotter than 4,000^c there.

The shining sun
A fiery red lights the horizon,
Formed into a beautiful sunset.

Joseph Tester (10)
Chesworth Junior School

THE SEA

Calm sea,
Glinting in the morning light,
After the roughness of the night.
Shimmering a turquoise blue,
Everything still, things scarcely move.
Boats drift slowly to the shore,
Water silent from the ocean floor.
Calm sea.

Wild sea,
Vast waves under a stormy sky,
The sand on the beach is wet where it once was dry.
Hear the wind's furious roar,
Violent from the ocean floor.
Boats struggle over the massive waves,
Wild sea.

Stephanie Barr (10)
Chesworth Junior School

A DAY IN THE PARK

Swinging on the swing,
Jumping on the slide
Slither down like a snake.
Dogs dodge the grass as they run from side to side,
Having a picnic, picking peanuts from the bag.

Footballers kicking balls in the air,
Down to somebody's feet.
Squirrels jumping from tree to tree,
As fast as they can go
Children slide down the fireman's pole laughing all the way.

Bees buzzing, collecting pollen,
Wasps whizzing, landing on your food.
The leaves of the trees shine brightly,
Flowers start to grow,
Ducks quacking for more bread.

Oh! It has started to rain!

Jack West (8)
Chesworth Junior School

THE STORM

The wild storm rages on like an angry giant,
Yellow lightning, bolts through the sky like fiery weapons,
As its thunderous voice shouts and echoes furiously.
The wind shrieks loudly like a pterodactyl,
Its icy feet grip the house as tightly as a brick in the wall.
The rain beats incessantly against the window like a hammer.
Inside, the fire greets us like the sun on a hot day.

The rain fills the streets with rugged floods,
Driving people out of their ruined homes.
Trees forced to the ground making noises that spread far and wide.
Big *bangs* of thunder make people jump!
Lights whisper, then poof, a blackout has begun.
Nobody knows where they are, families huddle to keep each
other warm.
Shed roofs flying from garden to garden.
Don't go outside,
The storm is horrendous.

Nicholas Reeves (11)
Chesworth Junior School

STILL AS STONE

An old stone gargoyle
On the top of an old marble pillar
At the edge of loneliness
With not a friend in the world
Gazing out sadly over the ruined houses that were once homes.

An icicle
Hanging on the tip of a mountain
Never to drop
But always to hang.

A fashion dummy
In a deserted clothes shop
Waiting in a time like forever
For when it will be demolished.

Jack McGearty (9)
Chesworth Junior School

WHAT AM I?

What am I?
What do you think?
Go on try and think.

I could be black,
I could be brown,
I could be any colour except a bright one!

I might be fat,
I might be small,
I won't be tall,
But we all start off very small!

Inside it seems to be full of things,
Bikes, trikes, spades and things.
I climb up onto a large box type thing,
Which seems to be humming!
Ooh ha, at last something nice and soft to rest my bot.
I curl and sleep until it's time to eat.

Have you guessed what I am?
Yes, you are right, I am a dog!
With a lovely life, sitting, eating in my shed!
Woof, woof, woof!

Megan Hoskins (10)
Chesworth Junior School

ADVENTURE WORLD

Open up a big box
Bouncy ball inside
Pouncing and dancing around the house
Flubbery moves to get higher in the air
Roll around on the floor rough and bumpy
Seeing the world around me
I can't stop rolling and I keep bumping into other toys
Open the door out I go
Under the cars that zoom past me to make me go faster
Rolling past houses and gardens too
Frightful trains and zooming aeroplanes
High up in the never-ending sky
Children kicking me further away
To see many different things in many different places
Gliding past trees and flowing down streams
A supersonic ball with wheels and extra power
To make me blast past everything
Too fast to even see where I'm going
With the wind blowing on my face
I feel like a rocket blasting into space with all my air gone
I'm rolling into a garden I've seen before
Travel into the house and there's my owner
Now I'm in a warm home, in a warm bath being
Cleaned from all that mud and dirt.

How lovely!

Samantha Beckwith (9)
Chesworth Junior School

KARATE

I was woken Sunday morning,
By my alarm clock ringing loud.
I had to go to Manchester to join the karate crowd.

The mini bus arrived at 5,
And we were on our way,
We were very tired but excited about the day!

We had to stop to have a break,
We had coffee and a cake.
But soon we were back on our way,
To the competition, hip hip hooray.

We arrived at 10 o'clock and said
'At last we're here!'
To the boot we had to go, to get our karate gear.
Into the hall we made our way
Poor old Dad he had to pay.

On with my kit, I was ready to go,
I was very nervous, I hope it didn't show.
My name was called, to show my kata,
All I could hear was my heart's pitter-patter.

I did my best and Dad was proud,
I heard the clapping from the crowd.
We're on our way to end the day,
Off again down the motorway.

Stacey Cattermole (9)
Chesworth Junior School

A BIKE RIDE!

Zoom, zoom!
As you brush past the trees

Zoom, crack
As your bike kicks up the leaves

Zoom, fly
As you jump off a mud ramp

Zoom, splash
As you land in a deep, muddy puddle

Zoom, crash!
As you hit your dad's car!

Matthew Clark (10)
Chesworth Junior School

THE WISE OLD OWL

The owl is a wise and quiet bird,
He sits on a branch all day and dreams,
About going to places nobody has been before,
And meeting a beautiful companion.

The owl is a wise and quiet bird,
At night he silently flies through the starlit wood,
And carefully looks for field mice and rats,
Suddenly he sees a movement in the grass and opens his claws,
He has caught a plump rat.

Laura West (9)
Chesworth Junior School

THE POET

A poet
most of the time
uses something
that does rhyme.
But sometimes
no rhymes
consist
in the poem.

A poet
mostly uses
something
that amuses.
All must be his
that is
amusing
in the poem.

David Nicholas (10)
Chesworth Junior School

RAIN

R   ainbow where the sun shines,
A   norak when it's pouring,
I   ce when it freezes,
N   atural as the rain.

Philippa Croucher (7)
Chesworth Junior School

FOOTBALL DREAM

My greatest dream is to play for England.
To be a superstar.
To walk out onto the pitch.
To hear the sounds of cheers and roars of
'England, England' for the cup.

The anthem plays and the whistle blows,
The match begins.
My glory comes when I score the winning goal!
The players jump and run with joy.
From the crowd comes the sounds of
'Roadley, Roadley, superstar!'

Harry Roadley (9)
Chesworth Junior School

THE RACE

Heart is pumping,
Pulse is racing.
I see the trophy I am chasing.
On your marks, get set, go!
Oh no, I'm too slow!

The finish line is now in sight,
I must try with all my might.
The crowds all cheer, 'Number three!'
The winner, yes, that is me!

Justine Thompson (8)
Chesworth Junior School

THE DANGERS OF THE GARDEN JUNGLE

Out in the garden, if unlucky, you will see
A great golden tiger (with Tibbles on his collar)
Just waiting to pounce

Beware! Beware! Don't go outside!

Watch out for the deep waters of the fishpond
Although the fish look harmless they really are piranhas!
A dish of human is pleasing to these Amazon fish

Beware! Beware! Don't go outside!

Beside the pond of piranhas there sits a bearded man
Threatening you with his stick, he's fishing for his tribe
(And by the way, if you don't know, the tribe is called the Gnomes)

Beware! Beware! Don't go outside!

If you now take refuge in the safe-seeming flower bed
Look out! A killer's on the scene! A thousand brave explorers
Have fallen victim to the red flower's deadly thorns

Beware! Beware! Don't go outside!

A child's play toy doesn't seem a likely death
But the quicksand pit, full of buckets and spades
Has become the greatest danger!

Beware! Beware! Don't go outside!

So take my advice, forget the garden
Please don't go outside
Stay in and play, just don't go outside

Beware! Beware! Don't go outside!

Maria Grainger (11)
Chesworth Junior School

HATE THE RAIN

'Hate the rain'
said the boy
with the mud
in his eye.
Soggy boots,
chilly legs,
boggy pants.

'Hate the rain'
said the boy
as he shot
skidded wide,
to the laughs
and the shouts
and the chants.

'Give me rain
in my hair,'
said the boy
in the chair.
'Give me mud
on my boots
and in my face.

Give me one
chance to play.
Just five seconds,
some day.
Just one kick,
just one touch.
In your place.'

Nicholas Purtill (9)
Chesworth Junior School

CLIMBING MOUNT EVEREST

Day one, driving there
Hour by hour
Minute by minute.
When will we get there?

Day two, got to the bottom at last,
Icy and cold
Not dry, but wet.
Miserable and soggy.

Day three, started to climb,
Getting windier and windier,
Can't feel my fingers
Or toes.

Day four, I'm starving,
I could eat five horses
Including their riders.
Oh, when will we eat?

Day five, nearly at the top,
Still wet and cold
Miserable too.
Oh, it's so cold!

Day six, I miss my mum,
Dad too,
And my sister.
Cat and dog too.

Day seven, last day of the week,
I've eaten,
I've drank.
I can't believe it, we're there!

Abbey Swansborough (9)
Chesworth Junior School

HORRIBLE HOMEWORK

I always say, oh why do I have to do my horrible homework?
I always want to throw it in the bin.
Oh why do I have to do my horrible homework?
English, science and maths are boring.
I'd rather play on the computer.
Oh why do I have to do my horrible homework?
I'm always itching about in my chair.
I'd rather make a spyhole in the tree.
Oh why do I have to do my horrible homework?
I'd rather be making traps for my sisters,
Oh why do I have to do my horrible homework?
I'd rather be flying a plane
Than doing my
Horrible, horrible
Homework!

David Rowland (9)
Chesworth Junior School

LOOK WITHIN

Look within my eyes,
Look within your future.
What do you see?
Nothing . . . nothing.
There's just a blank space
Where no one's living.

. . . Beware the voices!

Rayah Badman (10)
Chesworth Junior School

PLACE CAPSULE

I've just made a capsule,
A 'place capsule' is its name.
Just type in the destination
And in a flash of light, you are there.

I decided to go to the rainforest,
Damp and warm and moist,
The calm cool rainforest,
Dazzled by the blazing hot sun.

I have had enough of the amazing rainforest,
I decide I want a change,
I get inside the capsule
And type in my next adventure.

I next visit the ocean
And see a wonderful breathtaking sight,
Pods of dolphins and schools of tropical fish
Swimming effortlessly through the calm, cool waters.

I want another change,
But my mind is a whirling computer, full of ideas.
Greece, Florida and Blackpool in my mind,
But I am going to the moon.

The moon is a rocky cliff, standing in space,
Full of holes and bumps.
But up here there is *no* atmosphere
I *have* to go back to Earth.

I am now in my back garden
With flowers galore,
My adventure was a great one,
But I am glad to be home once more.

Alexander White (10)
East Preston Junior School

WIN BEETLE WIN

The engine roars as I start it up
Brrrm, brrrm! Off I go down the road
With my precious Beetle on the back
Past the trees and people, cars and houses too.

We're there now, at Goodwood racing track
I'd better drive my Beetle into the paddock
So I can get it ready to race.

Oh no! The tyre's flat and I should be on the track
I'll have to change it; I have no choice,
I can't let my supporters down.

Nearly done it! . . . There! I've done it.
I've got to be quick, the race is about to start.

I've made it just in time
'Ready . . . Steady . . . *Bang! Go!'*
I'm off; I'm in second place
Yes! I've overtaken that Porsche 911
Whey! I'm in first place!

Just one more lap then I've won the race
I've got to stay in front.
Oh no! That Jaguar XK8 has nearly overtaken me
If I speed up, I might just make it

'Win Beetle win!' shout the supporters
There's the finish line, I've won the race.
My supporters cheer and cheer
Well done! Beetle you're a star.

Jo-Anna Dockree (10)
East Preston Junior School

THE JOURNEY

It's time to go,
the wind is blowing
it's time to go.
The winged creatures
set off on their long journey.
Wings flapping as they soar
into the puffy clouds
perched upon the bright blue sky.
The creatures set off towards the south,
soon they lose sight of the green fields of corn
and the big old trees, they had nested in that summer.
They fly over the sparkling blue sea,
and at last they reach the hot sun of the south.
The journey is over.

Andrew Longhurst (9)
East Preston Junior School

SHOOTING STAR DREAM

Planets, planets is all I can see
Feet feeling hot, flying quickly.

Zooming stars
Flash of light
Dust, colours
Dreamy night.

Slam, wham, clam
Fall to the floor.
I wake up, but no more.

Jessica French (8)
East Preston Junior School

FLYING OVER LONDON

Flying over London, what can I see?
I see Big Ben and three restaurants,
Can I have some tea?
I see the London Eye moving at the
Speed of a tortoise!
Flying over London, what can I hear?
There's the noisy dome, it was better last year.
Big Ben's dinging as loud as a lion's roar!
Flying over London, what can I smell?
Something so nice, I nearly fell.
But the gas is as smelly as a garbage bin!
Flying over London, I see more.
So much to see, I need a tour.
I see the Houses of Parliament, standing so still.
Flying over London, it's time to land.
I'm so hot, I must be tanned!
I want to go back up, I demand!

Rowena Heal (9)
East Preston Junior School

FLYING SOUTH

I set off higher and higher
Soaring through the cloudless sky
Like a speeding arrow.
I am going south for the winter,
I've got caught in a powerful storm.
Eventually the storm cleared and I found
Myself in an exotic country.
My flying adventure is over!

Luke Gladdish (10)
East Preston Junior School

FOX SCAMPER, FOX RUN,

Fox scamper, fox run
Fox push those powerful legs.
Pounce off to your home.
Extinction has come.

The humans are here
They're slicing your house,
No time to sit around.
Don't stop for a tiny mouse.

Pounce to the river
Gallop to the water's edge.
Don't stop till you get there.
Now for the hard bit, swim!

Splashing down the river,
Disgusting smells of slobbery.
Splish, splash, splish, splash,
Till green land and grass come.

There's no food to eat,
The conditions are as bad as in a drought.
Fox you've been out for days
But the adventure has not gone.

At last green grass is here.
A nature reserve he has found,
Safe for centuries to come.
Now for time to rest.

Lee Finch (9)
East Preston Junior School

SLEEPING ON CAKE

I was catching a first class train
To Washington DC
To see George Bush (my grandad)
He was the President of the United States of America.
I am Luke Bush
My dad was Jim Bush.

A first class ticket
Said it was for tomorrow.
A party from Grandad to me
Yes please!

On the train, order a cake
Sleep on the shining chair.
I remember those beautiful chairs
And everything.

In sleep the cake came right beside me
So close
It felt like a metal bar
Attached to my side.

I rolled on it
Slowly and slug-like to the kitchen.
Awakening
Mysteries, it's all changed.
Surprised, astonished, amazed.

Searching . . . chocolate cake quest.

Next door chef's uniforms
Timespan spinning on, taking too long.

Abandon search, sit till end of journey.
Jump out of the train on to platform.
Scared Grandad whilst he was looking at the
First class section.
Went home happy ever after
To the White House in a limousine
To have a party.

Kailan May (10)
East Preston Junior School

UP, UP AND AWAY

Floating away up in the sky
Beautiful big balloon
Rock, rock from side to side
A dreaming fantasy
Down I go
Floating past balloons like clouds.

Far in front
Other great balloons
Peeping out from behind the clouds.

Down below I can see
Pinpricks of people, just like me.
Running and playing
Cows in the fields munching grass
Horses galloping on the downs
Fields like patchwork quilts.

Verity Stuart-Thompson (9)
East Preston Junior School

ON THE AEROPLANE

As the aeroplane goes up into the air
it jumps up and down like a hare.
Going along, steady and still
it doesn't make you feel ill.

As I see rivers flowing by
mountains are very high.
I can see cows and sheep
all bundled up in a heap.

I can see very wet washing
hanging from the line.
And lots and lots of people
chopping up pine.

I am sitting in my seat humming
Oh, dinner's coming!
After lunch, time for a sleep
looking down, it's very deep.

Landing time, getting off the plane
in the building, on the table is a stain.
Going home in the car
home from holiday we are.

Sarah Longhurst (7)
East Preston Junior School

HAIKU SEASONS

Now buds are blooming
Friendship spreading throughout Earth
Spreading joy to all

Now hot days have come
Buds and seeds have bloomed to leaves
Bring a nice cold drink

Cold days are coming
So why don't you wrap up warm
Or you will freeze up

It's the coldest now
So put your woolly hats on
Or be an ice cube.

Nathan Lavender (10)
East Preston Junior School

A DAY ON A BICYCLE

I pounce on my bike and speed into the road
Zooming, madly zooming
Dashing around
Riding down the road at a very fast pace
Lots of people with little blurry outlines
Dashing behind me, onto my back
Turning, turning
Left, right

Seeing crazy cars driving down the road
The wind whipping in my face
Dogs and cats
Mice and rats
It's getting dark, now getting late
Oh look! There's the front gate!
Slowing down, slower still
Gentle halt and in for tea!

My bike is resting, tired from its ride
Sleeping in its little shed
Having a rest, resting in peace
Waiting for tomorrow!

Daniel Hills (9)
East Preston Junior School

MOTORBIKE

On a motorbike from home I started to go,
Then I saw a bird flying
Singing, loving, kissing, tomorrow
People playing everywhere.

Chattering, fighting, hiking so there
Then I smelt the fresh air.
Sunny, warm air everywhere,
I saw the seaside.

Sand, waves, people swimming,
I saw blossom.
Fresh flowers, grass and oak,
I felt the warm breeze.

Nice, lovely, touching.
Yippee! I'm home again whoopee!
Off to work, here we go!
And home again (oh no!).

Nicole Kelleway (8)
East Preston Junior School

POETIC VOYAGES

Up, down
Round and round
Zoom, zoom, zoom!
Aah! Aah!
Faster than that car
Zoom, zoom, zoom!
Oh cool the loop, the loop
Oh no! The dark tunnel
I feel sick.

David Nicholls (8)
East Preston Junior School

SUBMARINE

Rushing through the water
Well not very fast.
Dolphins are swimming
So is a shark.
I can see a seahorse
I can see a fish.
I can see everything
Except it's on a dish.
I am in a submarine
But you probably knew.
I can see a fish
Glad I met you.
Squids whizz through the water
Into the darkness
Of their caves.
I can see fish eating what I gave

Amie Heath (8)
East Preston Junior School

FROM A CAR

Zooming, zooming past everywhere
Crash into me, don't you dare!
Dashing down the motorway,
With super speed and rushing power,
Dashing down the *long* motorway.
Oh my gosh! We're going 90 miles per hour!
Gently slowing down now,
Nearly safe back home.
Past our next-door neighbour's house
And now, we are back home.

Naomi Livermore (8)
East Preston Junior School

JUPITER

The massive mouth of fire
Floating through space
The Cyclops back again to
Destroy everything in your
Face!

The still quiet planets
Sitting in despair
Trying not to be seen
In case he is aware
To gobble them up
Never to be seen again.

Quiet, still space
No planets to be seen
The Cyclops still to be
Awakened
From his thousand year
Sleep.

Luke Howard (11)
East Preston Junior School

PLUTO AND JUPITER

Pluto
A blue, cold marble
With a rocky surrounding
As cold as can be.

Jupiter
A big ball of fire
A big, thin ring around it
Goes very hot too.

Natassha Evans (11)
East Preston Junior School

THE PLANETS

A ball of water
And drowns the poor shiny sun
Then calms down again.

Leader of the gang,
The eye of the great person,
The dangerous killer.

The ring of the bride,
The colours of her white dress,
A very, very kind man.

The size of a frog,
The most beautiful of all,
But colour we don't know.

Josephine Leyton (10)
East Preston Junior School

I'M AN AEROPLANE

I'm on an aeroplane
And a very nice one.
It bumps and it humps
It thumps when it went up
And when it's in the air.

It was okay, but it tilts
It tilts when it's in the air.
I can see wobbly stuff
Down below and
I can see cars and houses,
Buildings and war machines.

Laura Medlock (8)
East Preston Junior School

FOUR PLANETS

Magnificent ball of gas
Excellent shade of orange
Burning the planets

Great ball of fire
Perishing in its eyeball
Mixed in its colours

Extraordinary rings
Lovely circular big tree
Amazing colour

Eight mini eyeballs
A landscape of turquoise blue
A circle of ice.

Joshua Carter (11)
East Preston Junior School

FIREBOLT

Broomstick flashing
Werewolves smashing
Three-headed dogs gnashing
Broomstick bolting
Unicorns moulting
Vampires' teeth are revolting.
Broomstick fire
The Phoenix flies higher
May I admire.
Boomslangs biting
Trolls fighting
Hagrid writing.

Andrew Rumbol (8)
East Preston Junior School

BALLOON IN THE AIR

Balloon in the air, over the town
and guess what it's doing? Bobbing up and down.
Wings flutter by with loads of beaks,
and look at the babies, those tiny peaks!

Into the cloud. Oooh! I feel blind,
where the wetness will find my mind.
If the cloud is wet and the sun is dry,
perhaps it will make us hot as we pass by.

I'm sure we'll have fun,
would you fancy a bun?
I love this ride, I hope you do,
'cause did you know - I love you too.

And now it's time to land,
where I can see a band.
Loads of people waiting for me.
Oh look, they've got some tea!

Tom Chamberlain (7)
East Preston Junior School

SATURN

Spinning round in space
A yellow hat in the sky
Spinning ball of gas

A planet and its moons
A few mini followers
Eight rings around it.

Edward Hussey (11)
East Preston Junior School

THE SOLAR SYSTEM

A baking surface
Like a massive ball on fire
Which looks like the moon

Red-hot burning bright
Like a thunder ball through space
Death trap in itself

A place to live on
Like a ball of cloudy rocks
Which fire oxygen

Giant ball with ring
16 mini followers
Which hate the giant.

With beautiful rings
Like a colourful rainbow
And shines like a star.

A huge blue planet
15 mini disciples
Which hate the giant.

Blue planet with ring
As blue as the deep blue sea
Wisdom from the space.

Furthest from the sun
As cold as a round ice cube
Which freezes the air.

A giant red ball
With dark rock and dusty grounds
A huge ball of luck.

Hayley Stern (11)
East Preston Junior School

SAIL AWAY

As we start to sail away from the lands
and valleys into the ocean to another country.
On the way I saw some dolphins
they were pretty cute.
Five minutes later I was in the Atlantic Ocean.
I saw some fish springing up and down
and there at the very bottom of the ocean
the starfish lay.

Lydia Clayton (8)
East Preston Junior School

THE PLANETS

A small rocky core
a horrid dull, murky grey
burning in the sun

The most liveliest
with just one friend to be with
although so alive.

A poisonous ball
circled by a ring of dust
towering on things

A hard metal core
surrounded by ice and gas
extremely cold.

A giant prison
of blistering red-hot heat
trapping everything.

A tiny dry place
next to some speeding missiles
cold enough to freeze.

A huge solid core
surrounded by poisonous
gasses - all alone.

A cold blue planet
only comets to be with
although so pretty.

Really far away
an only friend, half its size
although it is so small.

Joshua O'Connor-Wright (10)
East Preston Junior School

UP IN THE SKY

I'm on an aeroplane floating by - up so high.
I can see the grey and white clouds out of my eye.
Seeing tiny people, nowhere nearby
How wonderful it is up in the sky!
Floating near to the clouds
Seeing the river down beneath us.
I like it up in the sky very high.

Rebecca McGuinness (8)
East Preston Junior School

A Haiku Voyage Through Space

Yellow tennis ball
Although mighty king of light
Throwing light over.

Whizzing here and there
Orbiting round big brother
Lifeless like metal.

Hot boiling desert
Beautiful light in the night
And full of pink love.

Full of scents and smells
Only planet to live on
A world full of light.

Cold and dusty place
Deadly war of volcanoes
A lot to be learned.

A Cyclops of red
A mad killer in itsself
With sixteen small friends.

Water colour set
And rings that cost pounds alone
Make a masterpiece.

A sideways planet
Big undiscovered ice cube
Full of frozen gas.

The leader of green
A sapphire in the night sky
A king of blue sea.

A cold dwarf planet
A small ball of loneliness
A sour storm breeze.

Emma Uncles (10)
East Preston Junior School

UP IN SPACE

Shooting up like fireworks
Counting down from ten,
Taking up into the stars,
I can see Mars.
Rockets are very colourful
And pointy at the top,
Rattling, rolling and spinning.

Shiny, silvery, shivering stars,
Sitting in the air, there are stars,
Sitting everywhere.

Planets are different colours,
They are different sizes and shapes

Spacemen floating everywhere,
Flying in their silver suits,
Going over and under stars,
Night is falling, we are back on Earth,
My friends said they missed me
And now I can go to sleep.

Kristina Harris (8)
East Preston Junior School

A JOURNEY IN A SPACESHIP

I'm in my room, asleep in bed
the next thing I know a laser's
hit my head.
I got sucked up by a big wide plane
I fell back down
and came up again.

I'm up in the plane and
I'm spinning around
It feels like I'm going to fall
and hit the ground.
In the plane is a gooey alien
I don't think this a plane at all.

I looked out of the window and saw
the moon, it was as shiny as a spoon.
I thought I would see my house
but of course I couldn't.
and there is, umm . . . I think
it's the stars. In actual fact
it could be Mars.

I closed my eyes and opened
them again and
Oh! I was back in bed again!

Sam Denman (8)
East Preston Junior School

EARTH

Hell is very hot
Heaven is a place of hope
Earth is in-between.

Daniel Pleasance (11)
East Preston Junior School

SIGHTS OF THE SEA

Looking out of the window at the sights of the sea
Seeing lots of images, lots of images of me.

Hearing the seagulls scratch and cry
Seeing them swooping through the sky.

Watching the frothing and foaming waves
Crashing, crashing into all the caves.

The stink of seaweed and the salty sea air
The fumes of the ferry almost everywhere.

Contemplating the lives of tired travellers on their missions
As they wend their weary way towards their destinations.

Waiting and waiting for the journey to end
Hoping and hoping to see home again.

Juliette Grevett (8)
East Preston Junior School

FIVE PLANETS OF OUR SOLAR SYSTEM

The cold deep blue sea
So lonely, no rings at all
A huge baseball.

An orange pumpkin
A large ball of spinning gas
Explodes on itself.

A big ball of fluff
Blankets of white fluffy snow
Sweet rocky surface.

The largest planet
Many miles away from Earth
Molten rock and gas

The coldest planet
Colder than Antarctica
Like a large snowball.

Lucy Miller (10)
East Preston Junior School

THE PLANETS

Nearest to the sun
A ball of rock floats in space
Revolving round the sun

The hottest planet
Fiery orange ball of gas
Yet no followers

Inhabited place
Blue and white palace of kings
Destroyed by owner

A rocky ball spins
Described as a red planet
Next-door neighbour - Earth

Giant ball of gas
It's a huge one-eyed monster
Sixteen mini friends

Beautiful ice rings
Small patterns on the surface
Pretty, revolving

It's a big blue ball
A huge ice ball with small rings
Lovely in its way

Sometimes furthest out
It's another gas giant
Not nearly as big

A tiny rock ball
Its only friend, a shooting star
Though the richest pearl.

Tilly Williams (10)
East Preston Junior School

IN THE SOLAR SYSTEM

Far away planet
not too far to run and hide.
The planet is fit.

A crushing machine
the ogre, ready to eat.
Has a strategy.

A place in itself
never too greedy to eat.
He takes things to heart.

One evil devil
great warrior in battle.
He picks on people.

A great ball of fire
he's floating around in space.
Yes he's a bully.

Very cold planet
just too many rings to court.
Although not married.

A purple planet
captured itself in colour.
He is an artist.

Too cold to stand on
a big hydrogen planet.
He wears woolly coats.

One lovely planet
a dark window in the sky.
He is all alone.

Daniel Williams (10)
East Preston Junior School

PLANETS

Rocky shrivelled crust
No gaseous envelope
No hullabaloo.

Serene countenance.
Custard clouds of venom gas,
Deadly to mortals.

Vessel of winds,
Tomato ketchup swirls
Circling Cyclops.

A blue pearl spinning
A snowy world in itself,
A white rock circle.

Oliver Bellamy (10)
East Preston Junior School

THE AIR TRIP

Purring off into the sky,
There's the runway, say goodbye.

Oh, there is the town down below,
Can you hear them say hello?
Here's Big Ben going ding-dong,
Did you hear it? Now it's gone.

There's a train, it's very fast,
Did you see it? Now it's passed.
There's the airport, time to go,
See yer, you know.

Owain Heal (8)
East Preston Junior School

THE SOLAR SYSTEM

Boiling hot planet
twirling around the sun
just needs to slow down.

Small ball of hot gas
hard core getting in the way
close enough to Earth.

One small little moon
atmosphere of oxygen
going very slow.

Great big volcanoes
the hot ashes burning you
but then powerless

The one-eyed Cyclops
its thin lonely swirling ring
enormous planet.

The beautiful rings
70 servants following him
eaten by his moons.

Cold blue ball of gas
plenty of thin swirling rings
it's getting faster.

Different kinds of blue
they're arguing all the time
always really cold.

Freezing cold planet
icy blue winds around it
feeling all lonely.

Charlotte Fleming (10)
East Preston Junior School

THE EXCITING TRAIN

Horses galloping in open fields
Old museums with ancient shields
Graffittied planes are whizzing by
Wet washing blowing dry
Small blue jumpers with no sleeves
Big apple trees with no leaves
Pure green grass on the land
Children playing with loads of sand
Creepy shadows following behind
Clever teachers using their minds
People gobbling down dainty dinners
In a race people are winners
Dogs barking from the great pound
They're making a whole lot of sound
There's a man drinking a beer
Oh and there's a lady in second gear
On that bench there's a man snoring
There's another man being boring
A field full of fresh daisies
People wandering through the mazes
Every lake is frosty and frozen
In that centre pets are being chosen
A driver of another train
He wears a badge saying Wayne
Sun shining in the sky
Making plants healthy and dry
It's time to get off now, getting down
Bye-bye houses and bye-bye towns.

Sara Trott (8)
East Preston Junior School

FOUR PLANETS

One freezing planet
big enough to freeze your breath
A ball of cold ice.

One thin boiling ring
made of different colours
It is very hot.

A terrible gas
which will dissolve anything
And colour of blue.

A bright silver moon
only comes out at night-time
To shine out bright light.

Luke Hirst (11)
East Preston Junior School

AN AIR RIDE

Fluffy clouds floating fluffily in our way,
Oh, I wish they would float away.
The sea is lashing in a terrible strop,
Its rage is never going to stop.
Tiny buildings miles below,
The world goes by rapidly, not slow.
Little sparrows flocking by,
Frantically in the light blue sky.
The runway crawls nearer,
The wheels grab the ground,
We're out and we're walking around.

Sarah Healey (8)
East Preston Junior School

SEA SUBMARINE

Off the land into the sea.
Slippery fish that makes a bubble noise
like electric eels.
Giant squid, starfish,
cod and octopus.
Look out for the tiny creatures
on your journey such as
prawns, krill or plankton.
Hear the seagulls skimming
the waters as the submarine moves.
We chase shoals of fish as
I go on my journey.
We are now hauled up by a
rusty crane.

Alex Chamberlain (7)
East Preston Junior School

THE PLANET'S PERSONALITY

The most lovely soul
In the end of life shines brightly
The life burns with hate.

Storming gas ogre
An evil eye brings great fear
A small rocky core.

Alone without life
Dead with no population
Regrets all his sins.

Love is a good thing
Hate is the sin of all sins
This strange life has both.

Jonathon Martin (10)
East Preston Junior School

SPIDER

Fly-eater
Animal-beater
Pest-catcher
Quilt-patcher
Scary-hanger
Body-banger
Web-spinner
Food-winner
Crack-hider
Midnight-rider
Spooky-flyer
Continuous-liar
Poison-bearer
People-scarer
Hairy-scuttler
Blood-butler
Mini-pouncer
Death-announcer
Garden-climber
Massacre-chimer.

Niall Browne (10)
Greenway School

MOUNTAIN STORM

Ancient peaks, old and grey,
Pierce the sky on a summer's day.
Slim pine trees whisper where they grow,
Birds sing to weary travellers below.

Then silence sweeps over the mountains tall,
A tense, eerie peace spreads over all.
Ears erect like statues, animals stand,
Time stands still over the rocky land.

Huge teardrops of rain bash the ground dry,
Dynamic gusts of wind dart from the dreary sky.
While the first white snake hisses through the blackness above,
Stone giants wrestling, play push and shove.

Explosion subsides, daggers cease,
All around the sound of peace.
A multicoloured mirage appears in the sky,
And finally everything is dry.

Victoria Morris (10)
Greenway School

MY MUM'S HANDBAG

You should see my mum's handbag!
Full of old stuff
Pens and old make-up
Paper and fluff.

My sister's spare nappy
My brother's toy truck
Our dog Sam's spare collar
And a stone that brings luck.

I looked in that handbag
To find my blue pen
Guess what I found?
A toy plastic hen!

Kirsten Parnell (10)
Greenway School

AUTUMN

A sea of dewy leaves stretch before me,
Golden fields expand for miles,
The scent of burning leaves mingles with the crisp air,
Autumn has awoken.

The last swallows dart into leafy carpets,
Triumphing with a juicy worm,
The wet grass is riddled with conkers,
Cold air blasts across my face.

Hedgehogs snuggle down to their winter sleep,
Plants bow their heads as the wind bustles past,
Winter is dawning,
But autumn is still here.

Leaves flutter in the air,
Finally settling in a thick carpet,
Birds fly south,
For winter is here.

Sheran Owens (10)
Greenway School

MY ROOM!

My room is a tip
like a bomb has hit,
overdue homework
like a pit.
My room is a tip.

My room is a tip
like an explosion,
clothes and posters,
my toy station.
My room is a tip.

My room is a tip
like a rubbish bin,
magazines, computer games
my bag broken in.
My room is a tip.

Vanessa Pitt (11)
Greenway School

THE CAT

The cat sits like an Egyptian sphinx,
Still and quiet.
It moves like a flash of lightning,
Fast and blurred.
Its ears are like small furry satellite dishes,
Twitching this way and that.
Its eyes are like the Mona Lisa,
Following you everywhere.

The cat's purr is like the rumble of thunder,
Crashing in the night.
Its whiskers are like corn in a corn field,
Swaying in the wind.
Its tail is like a velvet brush,
Soft and gentle.
Its coat is like clumps of soft, grey moss,
Smooth and silky.

Christopher Kidd (10)
Greenway School

KENNINGS SPIDER

Saliva-spitter
Insect-hitter

Web-weaver
Fly-fever

Web-maker
Fly-taker

Human-scarer
Gut-tearer

Food-beggar
Bug-pegger

Insect-killer
Mouth-filler.

James Forbes-King (10)
Greenway School

CLOUDS AT WAR

In the purple summer sky
Night begins to come
After a long day ablaze
The sun's job is done.

But then all of a sudden
A far-off rumbling is heard
And as the trees start to shake
The clouds come to war.

And then the sky begins to close
And battle breaks out between the clouds
The trees are straining on their trunks
As the gale howls through their leaves.

Now the cloud armies clash
Sending volcano-like roars through the mountains
Rattling the pebbles in every hole, cave and hollow
And creaking the pylons for miles around.

And slowly now it begins to clear
The trees and plants stop dancing
And at last the clouds disappear
The pebbles and stones stop prancing.

In the distance a gleam of light stands tall.

The sun has won the war.

Tom Grounds (10)
Greenway School

MEG'S MAGIC PEG

I know a woman and her name is Meg,
She has a pet rabbit and a magic peg,
Even on the wettest days her washing always dries,
Cos when she uses her magic peg, it's as if there're sunny skies.

But drying is not all it does, it helps in other ways,
When it comes to dinner time the table cloth it lays,
It cleans up the salt and pepper, the mustard and the pies,
And when old Farmer Bob walks by he looks at her and sighs.

The other day was very sad,
And Meg the dear got very mad,
The rabbit ate Meg's magic peg,
She was so mad she broke its leg.

I know a woman, her name is Meg,
She has a pet rabbit with a broken leg,
It has a bandage with signatures on,
And is happily married to a man named John.

Alice Brewer (11)
Greenway School

THE CAT (SIMILE POEM)

The cat awoke purring like a steam engine coming ever closer,
With its eyes like two narrow slits glowing with contentment,
It sits up as majestically as a goddess on a golden cloud,
Moving its tail like a weed waving in the current of a river,
Its ears are like two very sharp, velvet blades,
With its whiskers like pins that have emerged from a pin cushion,
And when it moves away it's like a snake weaving through the
                                        undergrowth.

Emma Alderman (10)
Greenway School

DON'T TALK WITH YOUR MOUTH FULL

Warm bread, cold bread
Nor hot nor cold bread
Just right bread
Nothing but bread
Now repeat while eating the bread

Warm milk, cold milk
Nor hot nor cold milk
Just right milk
Nothing but milk
Now repeat while drinking the milk

Don't talk with your mouth full

Warm ice cream, cold ice cream
Nor hot nor cold ice cream
Just right ice cream
Nothing but ice cream
Now repeat while eating the ice cream

Don't talk with your mouth full

Warm Pepsi, cold Pepsi
Nor hot nor cold Pepsi
Just right Pepsi
Nothing but Pepsi
Now repeat while drinking the Pepsi

Don't talk with your mouth full

Warm chocolate, cold chocolate
Nor hot nor cold chocolate
Just right chocolate
Nothing but chocolate
Now repeat while eating chocolate

Don't talk with your mouth full.

Rosie Lynn (10)
Thornberry Middle School

SUMMER

S   un is shining really bright,
U   nder trees what a sight!
M   y sister is having a race
M   y mum is staring up into space.
E   veryone is having fun,
R   abbits are playing in the sun.

Natasha Woollacott (8)
Thornberry Middle School

HEAVEN

Why is Heaven in the sky
I do not know why
But when you go up there
You're sure to know why.

Crystal Mustchin (8)
Thornberry Middle School

THE BIRD THAT TOOK MY CLOTHES!

I was just standing there
When then I heard a bird
It was one that came down
And took my top and then came a herd!

They pecked at my trousers and
Then they took my hair
And then they took my shoes
And I was standing there bare!

They flew away to their lair
And everyone stared
And then they started taking photos
And I didn't care.

Because they put me in the paper
They put me in a magazine
They put me in a poster
Then in a limousine!

Hannah Potter (9)
Thornberry Middle School

RACING LIKE A CHAMPION

I started off at the age of ten
And I was about as fast as a hen!
I was only a beginner, but I gradually got quicker.
When I had my first win, I did it again and again,
Until I spun it and made a big *bang,* as if it sang.
It smashed, why it crashed, it flashed when it was smashed.
It went in flames as if it was playing games.

Martin Tullett (10)
Thornberry Middle School

GATWICK AIRPORT (NORTH TERMINAL)

Down at Gatwick airport,
Sits the transit train,
Sponsored by British Airways
Back and forward again.

Go into the airport,
See all the check-in desks,
Britannia, American Airlines,
British Airways are the best!

In the silver lifts,
Press the button up
'Let's go to Boots first!'
'What a lot of stuff.'

In the silver lifts
Press the button down
Dash past the security man
Through the departure lounge.

Go through the departure gates
Walk quickly down the ramp
Go through the aeroplane door
To where the lady waits.

Lorna Sherriff (9)
Thornberry Middle School

SHOOTING STARS

Shiny, glimmering shooting stars, shining bright,
makes the night come alight.
In the day they go away
it makes you feel dull and grey.

Stephanie Robinson (10)
Thornberry Middle School

ALIENS HAVE LANDED!

Aliens have landed,
Upon the flower bed,
You should have heard my uncle Peter,
For this is what he said:

'Aliens have landed, once again,
Aliens have landed, come to reign!'

Then far off in the corner came the voice of my old aunt:
'Oh, those silly, stupid aliens have spoilt that lovely plant!'

But Uncle Bill, the wrestler,
'The Undertaker' by name,
Strode out into the garden
And put the whole lot off the game!

So the 'silly, stupid' aliens went back up to Mars
And everybody celebrated in the public bars!

Kevin Withell (9)
Thornberry Middle School

TOPSY TURVY

I went to the pictures tomorrow,
To see a dead donkey die,
I pulled out my gun to stab him
And he kicked me a punch in the eye.

I went to the pictures tomorrow
And took a front seat at the back,
I fell from the pit to the gallery
And I was punched a kick in the stomach.

Darryl Clement (11)
Thornberry Middle School

MY BATH AND THE WATER

'Have your bath' my mum was shouting,
when I was already up a stair.
'Wash and clean yourself with soap'
but I shouted, 'It's not fair.'

I stormed up to the bathroom
and shut the door behind
and let out a wail of surprise
at what I did find.

The bath had overflowed
the water at my feet,
the water growing higher
and my big brother Pete,

Standing like a jelly
screaming out for help,
he tried pulling out the plug
and gave another yelp.

I hate my brother Pete,
him I'd like to batter,
so if he falls in the bath
it really doesn't matter.

'You fool!' he shouted across the room,
'You are making quite a din,'
but he paid for that dearly
when he happened to fall in.

Kristina Adamson (10)
Thornberry Middle School

EVER WONDERED?

Ever wondered what it's like to be a tomato
And to be chopped, boiled, peeled and skinned,
Just like a potato?
We have to turn our heads
When someone gets the dreaded knife!

Now my old runner bean
Has been cooked without her top
And now it's going to be my turn and . . .
Chop!
That's the end of my life!

Ayesha Travis (9)
Thornberry Middle School

SPACE

Imagine you were up in space,
Aliens flying all over the place.
Hitting pinyaras
All shapes and sizes
Winning loads of prizes.

Then we saw a spirit from Devon
Flying all the way to Heaven.
We followed them up
Then we tripped up
And fell all the way back down.

Parris Johnson (9)
Thornberry Middle School

THE MATCH

Every Sunday, it's just the same
We go on the pitch and play our game.
Sometimes it's more like rolling in mud
Ouch! I'm sure that was someone's stud.
Levi kicks the ball from afar
Oh no, it's hit the crossbar.
The parents stand on the line and cheer
I'm sure they'd rather be having a beer.
The manager shouts 'Late night Lee?'
Why's he always picking on me!
The other goalie rolls the ball like a bowl
Jack takes it up and scores a goal.
Daniel dives to save the ball
Well done, that would have been 1-1.
The final whistle goes, we've won the game
But we know next week, it'll be just the same.

Lee Hayman (9)
Thornberry Middle School

ANIMALS

Animals come in all shapes and sizes
Animals can be quite a surprise
Some animals can bite
Some animals can be alright
There are some animals you should not get
One of the animals is a kangaroo
As a pet.

Katie Mellish (10)
Thornberry Middle School

Happy, Sunny Days And Years

Sunny days and years,
to chop the grass with shears,
for children do have fears.

It's summertime and the flowers are blooming
with insects busily buzzing about the vines
and we are playing and shouting busily about the house
helping mums and dads before going out to play.

All day long for lovely sunny days and years
so come and play with the happy children
of the world today,
so happy, sunny days and years.

Emily Barton (9)
Thornberry Middle School

At The Vet's

William Shakespeare had a very cute pet
But one day he had to take it to the vet.

The vet said to sit in his chair
Because he had to leave his pet right there.

'He's safe with me' the vet said to William,
'But don't worry, he's a pet in a million.'

A rabbit or a dog or a kitten's in there
Or even a humongous killer bear.
A bird or a tadpole or a little squawking owl,
A frog or a hamster or a little baby cow!

Rhiannon Saunders (11)
Thornberry Middle School

THE ROMANS

The Romans were barmy,
Especially the army,
Caesar the maddest of all.
Their eyesight was hazy,
Because they were crazy,
But they conquered Britannia and Gaul!
Augustus Caesar,
Nero the Geezer,
All of them ruled over Rome.
After a while though,
The Brits gave a smile, oh
The Romans had travelled back home!

Simon Withell (11)
Thornberry Middle School

THE AUTUMN WIND

The summer wind is warm and calm,
The winter wind is biting and sharp,
The spring wind is soft and gentle,

But the wind I love the best,
Makes leaves fall on our heads.
It looks so beautiful;
A carpet of colourful leaves,
Is something you will adore.
The wind is like a human,
Picking all the flowers;
It's autumn.

Bryony Short (8)
Thornberry Middle School

WINTER

W hen there's frost in the air
I see the foxes' lairs
N asty winter is mean, many people have seen
T his is horrible
E at warm food
R est in winter.

Charlotte Adsett (9)
Thornberry Middle School

JUST ENOUGH

Just enough peas on my plate,
Just enough times that I'm late.
Just enough friends and just enough foes,
Just enough people that say 'No'.
Just enough people in this world,
Just enough cats in a whirl.

Daisy Adamson (8)
Thornberry Middle School

WHERE DO TEACHERS PICK THEIR NOSE?

Do teachers pick their nose
Down the street, down the road
When they speed at 150 miles an hour
Do they pick their nose?

Are they long, are they short?
They are black I know they are
Or they might have orange spots on
Do they really have spots on?

If you pick your nose
You will turn out like a teacher!
Grey hair like Mr Glockler - yuck!
Do you pick your nose?

Caroline Glockler (8)
Thornberry Middle School

THE WITCH

I saw a witch on a broomstick
Fly across the sky.

How does she do that?
I ask myself, I wonder why.

She swoops and dives
So graceful does she look.

I'm flying with her
But then I close my book.

Lucy Minor (8)
Thornberry Middle School

PLAYGROUND

Wet when rained,
Dry when sunny,
Full of equipment you can use.
Hopefully you won't lose,
If ever there's a fire,
That's where you'll go,
Hopefully, no, no, no.

Nicole Skinner (9)
Thornberry Middle School

I AM A . . .

I am a human,
Living nice and well;
I don't want to move,
It might be like Hell.

I am a race bicycle,
Alone in the shop;
Please, please, please,
Take me to the top.

I am a scooter,
Very new and fit;
I was for Christmas,
Now I'm riding on the grit.

I am an aeroplane,
Gliding through the sky;
I like flying,
Now it's time to go high!

I am a model car,
Used quite a lot;
I'm too tired and old now,
Please lose the plot!

I am a ferry,
Sailing along the sea;
I am very five star,
So people stay with *me!*

Benjamin Northrop (9)
Windmills County Junior School

THE RIVER

The river
  Is a snake
    A slippery
        body
    It slithers
   Through
 The jungle
   In silence
     Scales shining
         In the sun
       Like stars
   In the night
  But
    Its fangs
       Are poisonous
     And
   Deadly.

Nicole Gibson (11)
Windmills County Junior School

THE SCHOOL PLAYGROUND

Children running
Children screaming
Children shouting
Children crying
It drives all the teachers mad!
Children skip forwards and backwards
Children jump up and down
Children tripping over
It drives all the teachers mad!
I'm glad I'm not them!

Sarah Hartley (10)
Windmills County Junior School

THE MOPED

The moped scoots through the street
With its furry seat and varnished
Shell metal body.

As it drives through the streets
A cloud of black smoke
Fires out of the exhaust pipe

On its journey past the shops
It reflects in the windows
It swerves round corners
And easily round bends
Through the traffic lights
While cars have trouble

The moped comes to an old country road
The mod hits the speed pedal, sixty miles an hour,
Seventy miles an hour, eighty miles an hour
Finally it is on one hundred miles an hour
Racing down the road.

Then there is a traffic jam
The moped comes to a halt
And swerves round the cars.
Finally it's home for a rest
But tomorrow it's got to go
And show off because mopeds are best.

Conor Hale (10)
Windmills County Junior School

THE WAY A DRAGON TAKES FLIGHT

He wakes up from his lengthy slumber,
The last beam of sunlight, lights up his hidden cave.
He moves his scaly body,
A lick of flame comes out of his mouth.
Gradually, bit by bit, he clambers out of his hideaway cave.

His strong claws keep a good grip,
While he looks out into the orange sky,
The sun is just beginning to go down.
He can hear the waves crashing against the shore,
From his rocky mountain.

Scales glittering in the sunset,
He unfolds his tremendous wings and starts to flap.
Soon he is in a beat, whoosh! Whoosh! Whoosh!
He begins to run, faster and faster until . . .
He's gone!
Like a black figure on the distant horizon.

Miriam Kennedy (9)
Windmills County Junior School

MAGIC MAN

There was an old man with a beard,
Who did magic and acted quite weird.
He had to be quick while doing a trick,
Or his audience all disappeared.

There was an old man with a wand,
Who was a great fan of James Bond.
He clapped his hands as he looked in advance,
As in front of them stood James Bond.

Daisy Marsh (10)
Windmills County Junior School

IF I WAS

If I was an astronaut
I'd fly off into space,
But if there was a warm hole,
I'd be sucked off with no trace.

If I was a motorbiker
I would *rev* around the town,
If I saw an accident,
I would call the royal crown.

If I was a rally car driver
In the worldwide race
I would win the first one
And keep up the pace.

If I was a footballer
Racing down the wing,
Looking for the big defender,
Who they call the king.

If I was a basketballer
Seeking for a shot,
The boss would call a timeout bell
And we would plan the plot.

If I was a spy
And a friend of James Bond,
We would go on missions together
And find the Queen was conned.

If I was a jet pilot
I would shoot into the sky,
When I do the loop the loop,
I am flying very high.

If I was me
Then me I am,
Just the same old me,
For all I can.

Tom Richardson (10)
Windmills County Junior School

TRANSPORT

Transport goes around
And breaks down.

Motorbikes
Roaring around
Speeding everywhere
Lying down.

Rally cars
Flipping over
Ruined suspensions
Racing over the finish line.

Submarines
Diving down
Hiding for ages
Releasing torpedoes.

Space rockets
Losing fuel
Reaching for Mars
Saving you from comets.

Transport goes around
And breaks down.

Ashley Raim (9)
Windmills County Junior School

STARS

Bright
as little log fires on summer evenings
   Twinkling
like dewdrops in the morning sun
   Fires
that are never put out
   Shining
like a summer evening sun on water
   Shooting
like a snake jumping at its prey over the sky
   Waiting
like a cat hunting its prey
   Exploding
like an atomic bomb.

Simon Bartlett (10)
Windmills County Junior School

COMING HOME FROM HOLIDAY

Thinking back to the animals
Standing in a crowd
But now I'm in an aeroplane
Skimming through the clouds

Thinking back to all the food
And bumper cart rides too
The slippery water slides

Coming down for landing
It's all nearly done
Now I'm feeling lonelier
Than when it had begun.

Paul Blackham (10)
Windmills County Junior School

PAW PRINT

They jump up at you
and bark all night.
They lick you
to wake you up in the
morning.

These rascals
chew up your shoes
and steal your
dinner from your plate.

They jump up at you
and annoy you
until you go to bed.

Abigail Elkins (8)
Windmills County Junior School

THE SNAKE

Rustling grass
Like the purring of a cat.
Green and brown
A muddied army uniform.
The snake coils
Around the fragile neck
Suffocatingly warm.
White fingers tug
The pulsating body.
Then, still and cold
Wearing in death
The snake scarf.

Claire Elizabeth Varndell (11)
Windmills County Junior School

THE GHOST

The ghost is your memories
    Written in a diary
Bursting out
    You're lost in your time
The ghost haunts your brain
    Lurking underneath corners
You need help
    You've lost your mind
The ghost hates your soul
    Ripping it apart
Fear and anger
    Driven down your bones.
The ghost will never leave you
    When you've found its soul
Haunting forever more
    You're stuck with its eternal taunts
The ghost is in your fantasies
    Playing eerie mind games
Taunting your brain
    Your brain is ripped out
Peace at last!

Hayley Elphick (11)
Windmills County Junior School

MY BUTTERFLY

Butterflies
Colourful butterflies
Fluttering wings
Repeating a pattern.

Joanna Griffin (7)
Windmills County Junior School

THE STORM

Black clouds creep across the sky,
Like velvet releasing its creases.
The rain hits the windowpanes,
Like gravel against a wall.

The wind howls ferociously,
Like an abandoned puppy.
Lightning strikes again and again,
Flashing like a firework.

The music of the storm plays again,
A pair of cymbals bashed together.
It is a giant in a playhouse,
Knocking us down like toys.

Emma Hayter (10)
Windmills County Junior School

ANGER

Anger is . . .
Like terror in the eerie glow of the woods

Anger is . . .
Rage walking through me

Anger is . . .
Death creeping closer

Anger is . . .
Flames catching fire to your heart.

Ryan Cannell (10)
Windmills County Junior School

THE STORM

Clouds bubble up turning purple to red,
The sea goes still and silent,
All of a sudden there's a mighty roar,
Thunder comes upon us like a volcanic eruption.

Lightning stabs into the gloomy night sky,
Streaking across the land like a trail of fairy lights.
Rain falls hard as nails,
Glinting in the bright, warm street lamp.

Slowly down come fences, trees and gates,
Scattering across the cold, wet path,
Blocking the way of an animal's den,
Its whine is broken by the howling gale.

After its damage, the wind moves on,
The rain stops pelting down,
Lightning stops striking across the dull, grey sky
And the sun begins to spread its wavy arms.

'The storm is over' sing the weary birds,
As they fly over the tattered town,
With bits of tree and fence strewn over the road,
'The storm is over' they cry!

Emma Speer (11)
Windmills County Junior School

WHAT CAN YOU SEE ON YOUR SWING

'What can you see on your swing?'
'Well I can see fleas, bees and apple trees'
'What can you see on your swing?'
'Well I can see figs, birds and palm trees.'

Charlotte Rider (8)
Windmills County Junior School

POND PARADISE

In the middle of a mountain full of lush sunlit poppies
A pond lay peaceful and calm,
The surface shimmered like a carpet of stardust
And flourishing lily pads floated restfully.

At the edge of the pond among the mossy rocks
Reeds swayed back and forth
And lazily the heron circles above
Peering at the darting minnows below.

The waterfall trickled and sung the sleepy lullaby
Of a stringed harp
Steadily the sleek, jewelled dragonfly hovered
And calmly the airy clouds in the tinted blue sky
Drifted off to the pleasant Land of Nod.

Danielle Page (11)
Windmills County Junior School

MEDUSA THE GORGON

Medusa the gorgon, she lives alone,
but if you look directly at her face
you will turn to stone.

Medusa the gorgon has serpents for hair,
she has two-headed dogs outside
but she has no sense of care.

Medusa the gorgon fires a bow and arrow
at those who enter her cave
which is very narrow.

Sam Hayter (8)
Windmills County Junior School

SUNSHINE

Sunshine,
Dazzling gold coins
Rotating,
Revealing,
Tropical island yellow
Covering waves, velvet, blue, mellow.

> Ringlets of women's hair
> Against her chest, pale and fair
> In person
> Subtropical,
> Warm,
> The enemy of a thunderstorm.

Morning song of a lark,
Pleasant as you wake
Rare diamond jewels
Luminescent,
Incandescent
Existing silently in deadpan, mute, inky caves.

Ellie Groves (11)
Windmills County Junior School

MEDUSA THE GORGON

Medusa the gorgon has snakes for hair
If you stare into her eyes
You will be turned to stone.
Medusa the gorgon has a two-headed dog
Cerberus is his name.
Medusa the gorgon has arrows
To fire at her victims.

David Chad (7)
Windmills County Junior School

ICEBERGS

Icebergs,
Their bitter coldness,
Moving silently across the ocean . . .
Peaceful.
Like suds of foam drifting on an icy blue pond,
Relaxing aimlessly,
No problems in the world.
Like palaces of crystal, vivid in the sun,
Glinting.
As the light bounces off the surface of the water,
They wait,
Ice cubes in their own freezer.
They wait for nothing.
The towering giants of the great North Sea.

Naomi Morley (10)
Windmills County Junior School

DIAMONDS

When I see
Butterfly wings,
They remind me of
Diamond rings
Diamonds and crystals
Are special things,
They twinkle and sparkle
In the sunlight,
But I cannot see them
In the darkness of night,
I wish I could because
They are a beautiful sight.

Emma Ingarfield (7)
Windmills County Junior School

THE BIG BEAR

The big bear lives
Down in the woods
And has lots of friends
Who give him goods
Like honey, biscuits
And lots of tea
He loves everybody
Including me.

Jeffrey Liu (8)
Windmills County Junior School

PEGASUS

Pegasus the glimmering horse
is so beautiful of course.
Flies so high in the air
cannot see her anywhere.
Shining in the sun above
Pegasus is full of love.

Eleanor K G Thomson (7)
Windmills County Junior School

FROG

A fat, slimy frog
Jumping up and down, leaping
Big frog eats black flies.

Sean Saunders (8)
Windmills County Junior School

THE NAME OF THE NEW GAME

A game I want
But what is the name
Of this type of game?
It can't be the same
As another game.
So what is the name
Of this game?

Hannah Logan (7)
Windmills County Junior School

PIGS

When pigs get muddy, it's gross
When pigs oink, it's loud
I've never really liked pigs
They're grubby and muddy
And never wash,
Or clean their teeth.
The way pigs live
Is gross!

Sara Fullbrook (7)
Windmills County Junior School

MY PUPPY

Dotty is her name
Soft and cuddly Dalmatian
She sleeps on my bed.

Lianne Baker (8)
Windmills County Junior School

OUTSIDE

All the green trees
and the dripping rain
and when I fall over
all that goes to my knees is pain.
So we've germs, the soil and worms
and start to play a new game
but when Mum says 'Tea-time,'
we all say 'Oh' and I kick the goalpost
of the goal,
but when we finish all our tea
and I do a burp and say 'Pardon'
my mum lets us in the garden.
Then it's bedtime and off go my friends
and the day comes to an end.

James Cassidy (8)
Windmills County Junior School

FAIRIES

There're fairies in my garden
They come at dawn
They play sweet games upon the lawn

They fly amongst the flowers
And cast their magic powers

What a special crew
Sprinkling fairy dust upon the dew.

They leave at dusk with a warm goodbye
And if they do not return
I shall probably cry.

Hayley Maloney (8)
Windmills County Junior School

SNOW

Snow,
It's a large sheet of wool
spread across the country.
Soft, white and powdery on the first
day of winter.
Brown and slushy when people tread
all over it.
But everybody loves the snow!
Gloves, hats and scarves are worn
as we go sledging.
It's so cold that it stings.
Now the sun is out and all the snow is melting.
Still everybody loves
the snow!

Fay Lewis (10)
Windmills County Junior School

THE BEACH

The crashing sea waves,
Hide the yellow, sandy beach,
Everything lays still.

Kristina Scuse (9)
Windmills County Junior School

SQUIRRELS

Little squirrels run
Hide their nuts in the green grass
Run across the road.

Francesca Guratsky (8)
Windmills County Junior School

LEGO

I build with Lego
Space stations and racing cars
Star Wars and towers.

Matthew Carter (8)
Windmills County Junior School

THE BOILING SUN

The sun is shining,
It lights up the whole planet,
Soon it has to set.

Victoria Monson (9)
Windmills County Junior School

HAMSTERS

He is very small
He's beige, soft and cuddly too
But he sadly died.

Sophie Sutcliffe (9)
Windmills County Junior School

THE RABBIT

The rabbit was nice
The rabbit was getting fed
Then the rabbit slept.

Susan Bell (9)
Windmills County Junior School

THE MATCH

Stone Cold comes in first
Gets a steel chair, hits The Rock
Stone Cold wins the match.

Miles Page (8)
Windmills County Junior School

OWLS

Owls gliding in trees,
Hunting white mice all night long.
Owls sleep in the day.

Jack Groves (9)
Windmills County Junior School

WIND

Silvery, white ghost,
A horse riding through the clouds,
Blows north, south, east, west.

Emily Sutton (9)
Windmills County Junior School

BATTLESHIPS

Big, black battleships,
Down come crashing bombs, bang, hit,
Wiping out the ships.

Thomas Carr-Coleman (8)
Windmills County Junior School

THE CAT

What's that in the trees?
Too late it's at my knees.
I'd better run very fast,
Or I'll be its breakfast.

The tiger is a wild beast
And wants me to be its feast.
'No way I'm no snack,'
It's time for me to quickly pack.

Over the hills and far away,
This is a place I'd rather not stay,
Away from the jungle, that's my plea,
I never again want to see an oversized flea.

I'll run away to a city
And I'll get a kitty,
It will kill all the mice
And I'll treat it very nice.

James Carter (10)
Windmills County Junior School

OLD FACES

Wrinkles like snakes wriggling
across the skin.
Waves lapping against the chin.
Eyebrows fade like a misty day.
Spots - atomic bombs
ticking away the time.
Ears like dinghies floating
beside the warship.

William Whewell (10)
Windmills County Junior School

106

The Song Of The Mountain Bike

This is my one.
The bright gold one.
My favourite.
My BMX bike.
I leave my house . . .
I cross the road, go down the path
Near where the train goes.
Up the downs, through the muddy track.
Down the hills, into the pond.
I push on the pedals as hard as I can
I turn my bike round and start off again
I reach the road
I . . . slow . . . down
Cross . . . wait
Get off
Great ride
Wow!

Michael Mtonga (9)
Windmills County Junior School

Fire

Fire,
A devil's home flickering in the hot air.
Fire,
Like burning hot, raging anger.
Fire,
Roaring like a fearsome lion.
Fire,
Glowing hot ashes escaping from the flames.
Fire!

Florence Wild (11)
Windmills County Junior School

FROG

As green as can be
Sees a fly, out comes the tongue
The fly is inside.

Emily Langler (9)
Windmills County Junior School

SPRING

Spring is here at last
snowdrops coming, daffodils
feeling the wet grass.

Rosemary Cook (9)
Windmills County Junior School

KOALAS

Koalas climb trees,
They're not afraid of the dark,
They're very furry.

Kate Sinden (8)
Windmills County Junior School

INSECTS

Insects are little
And they're very cute and sweet
They're very tiny.

Adrienne Coles (9)
Windmills County Junior School

UNDERNEATH THE SEA

Underneath the sea
Ships lay firmly on the ground
We are going in.

Nicholas Awcock (9)
Windmills County Junior School

COWS

Cows eat sticky grass.
Rushing to get the tasty bit,
one gets left behind.

James Mullane (8)
Windmills County Junior School

NIGHT

Night, dark and gloomy
does not like the day at all
ghosts have their party.

Andrea Potts (8)
Windmills County Junior School

SPRING

Daffodils come out
Birds sing sweetly in the trees
Lambs dance in the grass.

Jennifer Tucker (9)
Windmills County Junior School

THE SONG OF THE QUAD BIKE

This is the one,
The bright red one,
My favourite one.
My quad bike starts,
Vrrm, vrrm,
Off the start,
Up the bridlepath, on the downs,
Over the hill, through the woods,
Into the muddy track,
Across the fields.
Round and round go the big, fat wheels,
Slowing down,
Near the road.
Cross . . . carefully,
Over a bump . . .
Stop . . .
Home.
Whissoo.

Daniel Boyce (9)
Windmills County Junior School

BUTTERFLY

Butterfly, butterfly
don't fly away
I love your wings.

So don't go away
I beg and I beg.

So don't fly away
because you're
beautiful.

You're just what I need
come off the flower
and come back to me.

Sophie Barker (8)
Windmills County Junior School

TIGER

As the tiger lay,
Against the velvet night,
Like thin flames shimmering in the sky,
Waiting for his prey.

His coat was a lacerated carcass,
Eyes gleaming like the moon,
Flickering from side to side,
Waiting for his prey.

Vivid-coloured bird peeking through feathers,
Screeching to the wind and wide open sky,
Padding death comes creeping,
As the tiger pierces the flock of feathers,
The screech of pain cries out.

Alex Camilleri (11)
Windmills County Junior School

CORAL SEAS AND WALLABIES

I spent Christmas on the plane
While you spent Christmas in the rain

I spent Christmas in the sun
While you were in the snow having fun

I was swimming in a coral sea
While you were snuggled up with a film on TV

I was learning about wallabies and kangaroos
You were in the classroom doing 2x2s.

Elizabeth Jordan (8)
Windmills County Junior School

RUSHING SQUIRRELS

Rushing squirrels go
running up and down the fence
hiding nuts and fruit.

Alexander Short (8)
Windmills County Junior School

OWLS

Owls hunt in the dark.
Owls sleep soundly through the day.
They are chestnut brown.

Michael Jarvis (9)
Windmills County Junior School

WINTER

Snow is falling fast
It is white, glacial outside
The snow is laying.

Lorna Burling (8)
Windmills County Junior School

TRAIN

Creaking and screeching,
Slowly moving down the track.
Black smoke pouring out.

Alice Spendley (9)
Windmills County Junior School

THE CORAL REEF

The beautiful sea
has the coral reef in it
clownfish swim around.

Naomi Dryland (9)
Windmills County Junior School

POETRY DAY

Poetry Day is a fun day
because you can write
now go and do it!

Harley Sayer (8)
Windmills County Junior School

SEASONS

Autumn leaves go brown,
in summer the sun rises,
spring brings the flowers.

Abigail Forbes (9)
Windmills County Junior School

TIGER

Creeps through the long grass,
Waving round his body bold,
Teeth as sharp as knives.

Holly Hodsoll (9)
Windmills County Junior School

THE SKATEBOARD

My skateboard, go, go, go,
Grab it from the porch,
Out of the door,
Jump on my board,
I'm off.
Up the hill, under the subway,
Echoing all around
It's great.
Under my arm, now up the steps
On again, past the pub, to the roundabout,
Across the road.
Wheee,
Down the street to the school.
I stop,
Get off,
Cross at the crossing,
I'm on again.

Whizzing past the shops,
Getting fast and faster
Till I get to the town,
Meet a friend,
Get off,
Stop,
Chat,
Great.

Peter Mason (10)
Windmills County Junior School

THE CHEETAH

Hiding in the grass,
Camouflaged like brass,
Getting ready to pounce,
Cos he only weighs an ounce.

As he sees his prey
His tail starts to sway,
As he stalks the good old prey . . .

Running left, running right,
Running through the trees,
Now his legs start to wheeze,
As he's running through a breeze.

Finally he gets his meat,
He finds it's a bit too sweet.

As he stops, he stops,
As he stops . . . he
As he . . . as he stops.

Time to rest, panting freely
Ha, ha, ha, ha, ha.

Jamie Wills (9)
Windmills County Junior School

ORANGE GORRANGE

There was a young boy called Gorrange
Who had a body like a Jaffa orange
He had thick skin and was juicy within
And came from the planet of Morrange.

Rebecca Hull (7)
Windmills County Junior School

FEAR

Fear is . . .

A thousand cockroaches scuttling towards you,
Shiny and crunchy.

Fear is . . .

Falling into a black hole,
That's never-ending.

Fear is . . .

Your worst nightmare,
In a wakeless, eternal sleep.

Fear is . . .

Being trapped in a coffin,
Your nails tearing to get out.

Fear looks like . . .

An overwhelming cloud,
With glinting yellow eyes.

Fear is . . .

Completely silent,
A snake coiled round my heart.

Benjamin Walmsley (10)
Windmills County Junior School

DARKNESS

Darkness cuts my power,
Only stars make the light.

Why isn't dark our enemy,
Kindness is in the sun.

But darkness in its depths,
It is only a little fear.

Darkness fights for the night,
But night comes and goes.

Hayley Hewett (10)
Windmills County Junior School

THE SLUG

I'm . . . a . . . slug,
I . . . move . . . so . . . slow,
I . . . make . . . a . . . trail,
A . . . silver . . . trail,
The . . . wind . . . blows . . . me . . . down,
The . . . wind . . . blows . . . me . . . down,
A . . . step,
A . . . splodge,
Splat!

Isabel Sensier (9)
Windmills County Junior School

CLOUDS

As gentle as rabbits' fur,
That floats away like a dream,
Like white gleaming soap bubbles
Like a tear duct holding the rain.
Like ships sailing across the sky,
Like ice cream melting!

Alice Monson (11)
Windmills County Junior School

THE ELEPHANT

An elephant carefully trundles by,
I don't really know if he caught my eye,
His tail is spinning round and round,
He's about four metres off the ground.

Thump, bump, he's a big lump!
He's too heavy to even jump!
The elephant spins his trunk in the air,
He's standing there without a care.

He's seen a lush green tree,
Wait a minute, he's found a flea!
He's just having a quick scratch
And it's left a bright patch!

His big grey head, peers round and around,
I wonder what he's found,
He's found an apple in a bucket,
I wonder if he'll crunch it or suck it!

Lauren Streeter (10)
Windmills County Junior School

PEREGRINE

The sharp hooked beak like a charioteer's knife
The black beady eyes on a rogue's headdress
Pointed talons like Robin Hood's arrows
                    always finding their prey
Feathers; blue grey like the sun on water
Legs; an old person's finger
Hovering, a black dot in the sky
A dive, fatal and sure.
The peregrine.

George Everest (10)
Windmills County Junior School

THE CHEETAH

I'm a cheetah, I live in a zoo,
I love people just like you.
I'm a cheetah, I run really fast,
Look at me as I go past.
Look at me through the bars,
You won't see any scars,
You'll only see my lovely spots,
As I knock over your drinking pots.
Sometimes I like to climb up trees
I'm lucky I don't get grazed knees.
I love to chase a little grey rabbit
I know it's not a very good habit
Just . . . you . . . wait and see.

Philippa Chafen (9)
Windmills County Junior School

MY BEST FRIEND

My best friend is Helen.
We love eating melon.
We love chocolate too.
We love singing together
and playing a lovely tune
on our recorder.
She is helpful and kind
and I can tell her
all my secrets.
I like my best friend
more than anyone else
in the school.

Holly Pearce (9)
Windmills County Junior School

THE SKY

If I looked up to the sky to wonder what it really is?
I wouldn't care if you told me the sun shines on the
atmosphere and makes a giant blue eyelid.

I don't care, I wouldn't wish to hear,
Because I dream wonderful dreams.

Like once the bright blue sky was a blueberry pie,
And the clouds were candyfloss
And the bright, blazing orangey sun,
Was a tropical-flavoured ice cream, yum, yum

And looking down from this feast in the air
The bright green, short grass was littered with gummy bears
And the tree trunks, chocolate dipped.

Oh if that could be true, what would we children do?

Would we climb a giant's ladder,
Allowed to go and gather
Handfuls of those candyfloss-lined clouds in a jar,
To bring home to Mama and Papa?

Would we giant spoon the sky pie,
Would we reach and bite the ice,
Would we gather up the gum bears
And chew the trees so nice?

I bet we would, I know we would,
Us million kids together.

But oh dear Lord, imagine the effect upon our weather!

We'd have no sun, we'd have no rain,
The ground would be bare, the forests all plain.
And all night long the moon would shine
With no chance to sit like this . . .

And look up above and listen carefully as you explain . . .

Just exactly what the sky does and is?

Helen Sewell (9)
Windmills County Junior School

THE WHITE MARE SONG

The thunderstorm begins
And the raindrops run down my back
I start to run, clickity-clack
The lightning flashes
So many splashes as the raindrops hit the pool
But I'm no fool
I do not stand and stare
I'm the white mare.

A tree stands far from me a beautiful tree
Shelter . . . it could be
I'll go and see
And I'll stay there
I'm the white mare.

The thunder bellows and I look above
And all I see is a snowy dove
With feathers' fair
And I'm the white mare.

Kathryn Fullbrook (10)
Windmills County Junior School

THE ELEPHANT

The elephant runs across the field
Fast, slow, what is the deal?
Mum's plants say goodbye
As the lumbering elephant passes by.

The elephant runs into the shed,
Smashing everything down with his big grey head,
Leaving rubble in the city
The elephant hasn't heard of pity,
His stomach starts to moan,
As he's nearly at his home,
Doesn't know what he's going to meet there,
As . . . he . . . goes . . . to . . . sleep there!
Aah!

Robert Dawson (10)
Windmills County Junior School

ANGER

You're walking with your friends and they start to annoy you,
So you ask them to stop but they just ignore you.
There's a tiny spark of rage ablaze in your mind,
You try to walk away but they follow behind.
The spark's turning to fire,
You tell them to stop but they reply with something dire.
They're doing it even more so you do something abrupt,
It's too late, you're about to erupt.

The fire inside you is like a firework,
Up and up and up and then it blows,
You try to keep your head but you lose control.

Christopher Clements (11)
Windmills County Junior School

THE CHEETAH

I am . . . the one
The fast one
The very fast one.

I run and run, ready to pounce
But it has . . . it's bounced.
Then I chase.
I am so fast.
I go straight past.
Then I hide . . . then I jump . . . and then I kill
In the enormous open field.
Then I had a terrific . . . feast.
On the great . . . beast.

George Speer (9)
Windmills County Junior School

THE FASTEST FERRARI

It's the one,
The favourite one
It's red
It's fast
It's not usually last
But when you see it
It goes over the speed limit
It's so quick-fit.
It goes like a ball of fire
Burns the tyres and
It's faster than the others
It's the one
It's my favourite one.

Thomas Counsell (9)
Windmills County Junior School

THE DEVIL'S FRIEND

Anger is a dragon snorting flames of fire
Burning everything around it
Including the loved memories
That were once worshipped.

It's a volcano, boiling hot inside,
Waiting before it erupts,
It will never be forgotten,
The ashes are left for ever.

Anger is a bomb ticking in a room.
When it explodes it will ruin fondness and friendship
That would have lasted for eternity.

It's a lion that couldn't catch his prey
Starving, wild and mad,
Learn how to be a better hunter
Then rest gently in the shade.

Nicola Hobbs (10)
Windmills County Junior School

FIRE

Fire is like
a burning engine.
It looks like hair fluttering
in the wind,
moving constantly.
Like a forest fire
it sizzles like a snake in the desert.
Like a plane burning fuel
you can smell it on the air,
you can feel it in the air - hot, menacing.

James Goering (11)
Windmills County Junior School

THE BIG RACE

To the starting line and the lights are red,
Twelve cars lined up and the pace is intense
Then the lights go to green and they're off.
It has started to rain, slowly at first,
and harder and harder and faster and faster.
Round the corner and past the trees,
cars skidding, people screaming, barriers falling.
To the pit stop, cars refuelled and tyres changed.
and they're off again.
It's the third lap,
faster and faster with skid marks everywhere.
The cars race on lap after lap.
Porsche No 2 is ahead, closely chased by Ferrari No 7.
Who will win?
Porsche? Ferrari? Bennetton?
No, Porsche No 2.
Hurray!

Alastair Holmes (9)
Windmills County Junior School

TEN THINGS YOU WOULD FIND IN MUM'S BAG

A snotty old tissue from my younger sister,
A plastic bag with an old banana skin and loads more mouldy stuff.
One bottle of whisky,
Different perfumes which smelt like mouldy bins,
Three mirrors because they always break on her,
Mouldy chewing gum, three years old,
Five disgusting colours of lipsticks,
Mouldy mobile phones, with a pretty cover
A purse with no money in it,
Dad's lucky charm.

Katy Davey (10)
Windmills County Junior School

ELEPHANT POEM

I'm a big grey elephant
Listen you can hear me pant
In Africa
In India
I charge across the shaky ground
Rushing through the trees I go
Sandy, splashy water
I don't know
Run, run, never stop now,
Until I find an enemy, not a pal
Stop
There he is, the one with the tusks
Can I fight? Can I not?
Oh! Look he's turning around
So I'll just wait till he's found
Yawn
I can't . . . stay . . . awake . . .
Yawn . . . asleep.

Olivia Dawson (10)
Windmills County Junior School

BANANAS

Yellow like a baby canary
Sweet like candy
Slippery like soap
Long like an old rusty double-barrelled shotgun
Black as thick oil
Soft like clouds in Heaven
Moon-shaped like the corner of an ear.

Adrian Crees (11)
Windmills County Junior School

THE STORY OF THE MOTORBIKE

This is the one
That is the one
This is my only one
That is the red one
It's the motorbike
Out my house,
Past the park
Down the hill,
Very fast,
Up the bumps,
Through the field,
And it kills,
Over the bridge,
Through the tunnel,
I see my house,
Nearly there,
Nearly there,
Nearly there
There!

Jack Carter (9)
Windmills County Junior School

CANDYFLOSS

A pink cloud,
Hovering over a mountain,
Pierced by a stick,
Held imprisoned.
Sticky as a loner,
Trapped in a transparent skin.

Hannah Scuse (10)
Windmills County Junior School

SKIPPING

In the playground skipping
With my friends
I hope playtime never ends
Criss-cross, criss-cross,
Skip, skip, skip,
Forwards, backwards,
Double skipping with Naz.

It's my turn to jump and laugh
Around and around the rope goes fast
My feet barely touch the ground
Faster . . . faster
Rope in the way.
Game . . . over!

Georgia Hancock (9)
Windmills County Junior School

THE CHEETAH

I'm a cheetah,
A killing monster,
Heart pounding past.
Every time I'm in a race,
I'm never last.
A flashing thunder in the sky,
A little twinkle in my eye,
A beautiful grin on my face.
The race is on,
I'm starting to chase . . .

Nazia Zaman (10)
Windmills County Junior School

THE CATERPILLAR

In a lush green tree,
In a cool summer breeze,
On a light yellow leaf,
Lurks the caterpillar.

On a cold misty day,
On a fruitless tree,
With a sharp autumn breeze
Sleeps the caterpillar.

On an icy, snowy eve,
In-between the frosty leaves
On a warm, cosy bed
Sits the caterpillar.

On a warm, sunny morn
I wake up at dawn,
And look up at the sky
No longer am I green and thin,
I'm now a . . . butterfly.

Felicity Polden (10)
Windmills County Junior School

WATERFALL

Crashing, a landslide

A rumbling noise
Like shooting arrows being shot over a wall.
Falling like a bomb from a plane
Bubbles bubbling in a bath
Popping at every splash
Pounding like a stampede of elephants.

Christopher Fenwick (10)
Windmills County Junior School

NIGHT

Night is a monstrous wave,
Or maybe a husky black cat,
Every now and then you hear a moan,
Or even a flowing whisper.

When the lightning and thunder wake up,
Their rage billows and growls;
The monstrous wave of night,
Rocks in the gloomy black sky.

When I walk out into the night,
I'm always looking behind me,
Is someone following me
Or watching me in the dark?

Night is as misty as my dreams,
As starry as my hopes,
As frightening as my nightmares,
As renewing as happiness.

Sophie Gladman (11)
Windmills County Junior School

THE HEART OF FEAR IS . . .

When a thousand hands are reaching to grab you
And you're trapped with nowhere to go.
When lions are scratching you with their claws
That is the heart of fear.

When a spider on bristly legs is inching forward
And the thunder is crackling and crashing.
The stairs are creaking under your feet -
That is the heart of fear.

When icy winds pierce your back
And whistle around dark corners,
When a ball of fire is hurtling towards you
That is the heart of fear.

Laurie Holford (10)
Windmills County Junior School

WEATHER - BY A TORTOISE

The miniature snowballs falling down
Are peas for my dinner,
The colourful rainbow overhead
Is a giant slide for playtime.
The luminous sun, dangling up above
Is a spotlight for my performance.
The twinkling rain, trickling down
Is sapphires against my shell.
The whistling wind whirling around
Is a mammoth fan that cools me.
The furious thunderstorm, circling over me
Is an angry, bellowing bear.
The cotton wool clouds puffing over
Is a soft bed for me to snuggle up in.

Jenni Forshaw (10)
Windmills County Junior School

SNAKES

Slithering along
All day long he shakes his tail
The slithering snake.

Katie Gladman (9)
Windmills County Junior School

RATTLESNAKE

The snake awaits coiled in the swelling dunes,
Waiting patiently in the shimmering sun,
His yellow-speckled scales
Like the sand he glides across.
Long tongue, pronged like a barbecue fork,
Spiteful diamond eyes
Flickering from side to side.

He yawns, fangs like elephant tusks
Dripping venom he slithers towards a scent
That swerves away
A too frightened, cautious prey,
There is a silent death
By vampire bite
The oasis beckons, gleaming like the moon.

Oliver Fenwick (10)
Windmills County Junior School

FEAR

Fear is a thousand needles piercing you
A ball of fire zooming towards your heart
It is like being shut up in a coffin of darkness.

Fear is like touching the insides of your body
A spider scratching your spine
It is being struck down by thunder.

Fear is sweat running down your face
A demon on your back pulling you down
It is a snake sucking out blood.

Laurence Potts (10)
Windmills County Junior School

THE CAT

The cat has ears like sitting owls
A nose like a moth
Whiskers like strings of spaghetti
And a tail like a feather duster.

Deep in the cat's eyes lies the sheen of a butterfly's wings
Green, green eyes, but in shadow, a dark, smoky gold
Poised on silvery paws,
The cat sits gazing into the blue beyond.

A blazing fire, candles lit,
Curtains drawn, kettle boiling,
And finally the cat stretched out before you,
A scene of perfect harmony.

Alex Knight (11)
Windmills County Junior School

TEN THINGS IN A PRINCESS' BEDROOM

A brand new purple dress with gold ribbon and diamonds,
Lots of brand new crowns, all types.
A walking, talking four poster bed with glass each side,
Gold curtains with diamonds,
Some animals talking,
A princess' baby in a laughing cot,
A poster of Prince Charming on the wall,
A book called 'How To Make A Frog Into A Prince',
Some servants who look so pretty,
A pair of slippers with diamonds,
Lots of toys on the shelves.

Collette Churcher (10)
Windmills County Junior School

STORM

The trees swayed in the coal-black night,
The wind howled and hollered,
Lightning flashed, the thunder roared,
As my dream turned into a nightmare.

A dark, black cloud towered over me,
As whispers filled the room,
Cold shivers of pain ran up my back,
As the moon disappeared into the mist.

The night's gleaming stars looked down with a fright
As the rain came crashing down,
The hail shattered the windowpane,
As the cold, frosty breeze drew near.

Natasha Churchill (11)
Windmills County Junior School

TEN THINGS IN MY TEACHER'S DRAWER

A half-full bottle of vodka,
Anti-mad pills,
Chocolates with milk creme eggs and Mars bars.
Mobile phone with Bob the Builder phone cover,
A long list of chat-up lines,
A CD player with CDs
Some fake tattoos,
Letters that should have been given out two weeks ago,
Mouldy gum already chewed.
Ten yo-yos confiscated from class.

Nicola Burse (10)
Windmills County Junior School

DRAGONS

Dragons large and fierce
With raging flames,
Coming out of its mouth
And nostrils.

Dragons black and lumpy, bumpy
Tough scales and
Gleaming white teeth
That shine in the dark.

Dragons in dark
Creepy caves
Dragons in old ruined castles
High in the Welsh mountains
Feeding on wild animals
That pass if they dare.

Dean Howard (11)
Windmills County Junior School

THE STORM

Thunder is a pack of dogs
Growling as it echoes through the night.
Clouds of blood scattered across the sky.
The deep black anger of the sky, tinted with red.

Lightning flashes across the darkness
Like daggers being thrown down to Earth,
The pounding tears streaming down the sky's face.
While the wind moans through its mouth.

Sophie Whatford (11)
Windmills County Junior School

PREDATOR

Sun-drenched air, fresh and young
Pads against torn, ragged skin.
Deep red eyes, lava pits, stare intensely
Seeking a wanted blue vein.

Movement close by. Freeze. No motion now,
Steady, make ready for ambush. A pounce of life or death.

For a heartbeat, an intrigue, its own slyness
Its stealthy trickery, so proud, so foolish, for the prey will escape.

Attack. The pounding beat of sharp padded feet
Thumps against the dry blistered sand
Bullet speed drowns the quarry's flight
Collision, with the lusted tense flesh.

Razor claws like Samurai swords
Rips its innocent victim apart.
The volcano of blood erupts in a flood
Steaming sickly as it spreads through the sand.

Dennis Sewell (11)
Windmills County Junior School

SPACE

Space is a black hole which is eternal.
Space is a universe full of trapped fireflies, twinkling in the moonlight.
Space is a spectacular show of shooting stars and comets.
Space is agoraphobic black, a bottomless pit.
My senses reach to space so I can see it.
I am left amazed.

Aiden Janman (11)
Windmills County Junior School

FIRE!

Fire!
Fire is a burning tower
Glowing in the black,
Fire is a painful death
Boiling up my back.

The colours rise around us
Like candles in the dark,
Fire is a lit-up match
Leaving ashes as its mark.

Fire is a gleaming star
Flickering in the night,
Fire is a fireball
Causing a new-made light.

Beth Hulse (10)
Windmills County Junior School

CLOUD

Winter snowball in the air
'The cloud'
Fairs' candyfloss
Soft
'The cloud'
Stormy night
Black
'The cloud'
Steam train
Travelling across the sky
'The cloud'
A boat sailing across the sky
'The cloud'.

Matthew Freeman (11)
Windmills County Junior School

TEN THINGS YOU WOULD FIND IN A DRAGON'S CAVE

A fire extinguisher for accidental sneezing,
A half-eaten boy with head still attached,
A helmet and sword from a knight.
Lots of bones, assorted animals and humans.
Sore throat pastilles, dragons only, too strong for humans,
Mobile phone, dragons only, fireproof (innovation Nokia 3310).
A TV and video with the Fireman Sam complete collection
A magazine called 'Ten Ways To Help You Fly'.
A cleaning kit for jewels and gold,
A book called 'One Hundred Ways To Cook And Eat Humans'.

Daniel Short (11)
Windmills County Junior School

FIRE

Like sand burning on a hot day
Like a rainbow starting to appear
Like a snake being charmed out of its basket
Like flakes of dead skin spread on the floor
Like disco lights
Like a roaring oven
Like a home of a devil at dinner time.

Lucy-Anne Waddell (11)
Windmills County Junior School

THE SADNESS OF THE SEA

As I gaze at the sea lapping against the shore,
I stand and think what lies beyond the ocean,
Islands waiting to be discovered.
Fishes darting between the giant waves,
The sea is like a galloping horse,
Crashing onto a pebbly beach.

As I look at a boat in the distance,
I think what is under the ocean,
Seaweed squeezing between your toes when you walk,
Colourful coral that is soft on your feet
The sea is things from the past
That won't go away.

Rachel Hobbs (10)
Windmills County Junior School

TEN THINGS IN MY BAG (WHEN I'M A TEENAGER)

A pair of bent glasses,
Half-full bottle of vodka,
A spare dress for a sudden party,
A mobile phone to talk to boys on,
(With a Bagpuss cover).
Scott's number on the inside of the Bagpuss cover.
To do list (meet 5ive etc)
Ticket to E17 Club.
A ticket to see 5ive backstage,
Cash and credit cards.

Kaya Pemberton (10)
Windmills County Junior School

STARS

The sun when it has just come up
A firework exploding
A black velvet sky
With light shining through the holes
That have been cut in the fabric
A rattling, coiling snake.

Louise Dove (10)
Windmills County Junior School

BANANAS

A banana is a yellow sun,
It is a smile with a puppy's nose,
Inside it is as creamy as vanilla ice cream
With brown blotches which are Dalmatian spots.
Stringy like cats' whiskers,
As slippery as soap,
As sweet as candy,
Soft as marshmallows,
Squidgy as mud,
As rubbery as a rubber tyre.

Rebecca Markham (10)
Windmills County Junior School

SKY

Sky,
A blue river with white
Candyfloss clouds.
Sky,
As blue as the ocean
Sky,
Like the sea flowing to shore
Sky, sky.

Natalie Smith (10)
Windmills County Junior School

ANIMALS

Birds fly, rabbits hop,
Sheep have wool and eat grass too,
Cows eat sticky grass.

Victoria Taylor (9)
Windmills County Junior School